Objective Tests in Introductory Economics

D1744057

Vivian Anthony

Deputy Headmaster,
King's School, Macclesfield

HEINEMANN EDUCATIONAL BOOKS

Heinemann Educational Books Ltd

LONDON   EDINBURGH   MELBOURNE   AUCKLAND   TORONTO
HONG KONG   SINGAPORE   KUALA LUMPUR
IBADAN   NAIROBI   JOHANNESBURG
LUSAKA   NEW DELHI

Without answers ISBN 0 435 84014 2
With answers ISBN 0 435 84015 0

© Vivian Anthony 1975

First published 1975

Published by Heinemann Educational Books Ltd
48 Charles Street, London W1X 8AH
Printed in Great Britain by
Biddles of Guildford

Contents

Preface

Since Don Baron and I wrote *Objective Tests in Advanced Level Economics* there has been a growing demand for another book of objective tests designed for a slightly lower level of attainment. *Objective Tests in Introductory Economics* has been produced to fill this bill. Students in their first year of courses for 'A' level or ONC/D, or preparing for intermediate professional examinations will find questions suited to their needs in this book. It is also intended for those pupils nearing the end of their 'O' level and CSE courses. The questions generally increase in difficulty towards the end of each chapter, and the later chapters contain more difficult questions than the earlier chapters, so that some of the items will be quite suitable for more advanced candidates. My Upper VI Economics sets have tried out all of these questions as part of their revision course this year, and my Lower VI set have been most patient guinea-pigs in the first instance. My thanks are due to all my pupils for the improvements which have been suggested when discussing the questions with them.

From 1974 almost all the Examination Board will be using objective test questions in their Advanced Level examinations. Most of these questions will be of the multiple choice variety and for this reason I have concentrated on this kind. The student will however find items of other types—true/false, matching, missing words—to bring some variety and more interest to the testing. Inevitably there has been a good deal of discussion about objective testing and comparison with the traditional essay type examinations. In the Introduction to the Teachers' Book of *Objective Tests in Advanced Level Economics* there is a detailed examination of the theory of objective testing to which I refer those who want to examine the question further.

If teachers and students are to make the best use of this book the questions should be used not only for testing but also as a basis for the discussion which should follow each test. Successful item writing depends on the ability of the writer to communicate the question properly to the student. Sometimes lack of communication stems from lack of knowledge or understanding on the part of the student, sometimes it comes from lack of clarity on the part of the writer. I should be pleased to hear from teachers and students of ways in which the questions might be improved (or indeed corrected) for future editions.

1

THE LANGUAGE OF ECONOMICS

1. Economics is the science which studies how to:
   (a) make money
   (b) make the best use of our scarce resources
   (c) redistribute incomes to the working classes
   (d) give to people all that they want

2. Which of the following are *not* the direct concern of the economist:
   (i) the prohibition of drugs
   (ii) greater equality of opportunity in education
   (iii) the need for an effective third political party
   (iv) the prohibition of trade with 'unfriendly' nations
   (v) the introduction of V.A.T.
   (a) i, ii and iv (b) ii, iii, v (c) i, ii, iii, iv (d) all of them

3. In the theory of economics all decisions are based on:
   (a) normative judgements
   (b) the principle of opportunity cost
   (c) positive judgements
   (d) the need to create the greatest happiness of the greatest number

4. By 'opportunity cost' we mean:
   (a) the total amount paid to the factors used in production
   (b) what we have to pay for a good
   (c) the amount of other things we have to give up to obtain the thing we want
   (d) the money cost involved if we miss the chance to buy something

5. In the early stages of man's economic development self-sufficiency was probably the norm, but he came to limit the range of his activities because he found that he could produce more in this limited range. Below are listed some of the economic concepts which stem from this development. Which one is *not* valid?

   (a) The concept of Specialisation
   (b) The concept of Exchange
   (c) The concept of Barter
   (d) The concept of Depreciation

6. In which of the following ways can the economist best help society to appreciate the problem of pollution?

   (a) By emphasising the maximisation of profits
   (b) By calculating the social costs involved
   (c) By calculating the marginal cost of alternative disposal methods
   (d) By emphasising that economists only make positive judgements

7. Exchange is an important economic activity because:

   (a) it made possible the invention of money
   (b) it overcomes scarcity
   (c) it enables both parties to the exchange to increase their total utility
   (d) it relieves the consumer of the problem of choice

8. The problem of 'choice' arises from the fact that:

   (a) there are too many goods available and consumers become confused
   (b) there is too little information about what goods are available
   (c) people's incomes are too small to buy all things they want
   (d) the consumer's marginal utility declines as he increases his consumption of a good

9. We use the term 'utility' in economics to mean:

   (a) the satisfaction obtained from the consumption of a good or service
   (b) the usefulness of a good or service
   (c) that a particular commodity or service is a 'good buy'
   (d) that a consumer needs a particular commodity or service

10. Which of the following sentences makes the best use of the term 'scarce' in the economic sense?
    (a) The Burnley football club ground is so small that tickets for a big match there are always scarce
    (b) Water is a 'free' good because it is not scarce
    (c) All economic goods are scarce because their supply is insufficient to meet the demand for them
    (d) Economic goods are scarce because the opportunity cost of producing them is too low.

11. Pick out the *incorrect* statement from those below:
    (a) production is the creation of utilities
    (b) production can only take place if some element of all the factors of production is present
    (c) wealth is created by production
    (d) the productive process ends when the process of distribution begins

12. We say that economic decisions are made at the 'margin'. This means that:
    (a) there is a fixed line which divides, say, land, which is worth cultivating from that which is not worth cultivating
    (b) decisions of consumers are concerned with whether to consume a little more of this commodity or a little more of that. The point where the consumer decides to consume no more of that commodity is the margin
    (c) the margin is the hazy area in which we are not sure if production is worth while or not
    (d) the extra cost involved in producing more units is set against the total profit. If the total profit is greater than the marginal cost, production will take place

13. We use the term 'wealth' in economics to mean:
    (a) the total amount of money which a man has
    (b) the total stock of goods which have a money value
    (c) the total of all savings in the economy
    (d) the current value of all services rendered

14. Which of the following best describes the term 'economic resources'?

    (a) All the factors of production, i.e. land, labour, capital and enterprise
    (b) All the world's raw materials
    (c) The stock of man-made wealth
    (d) All the free gifts of nature which yield an income

15. Fill in the missing words from the terms given below:

The main object of economic activity is to overcome the problem of . [1] . Our success in this activity is indicated by the amount of . [2] . we create. This is created by the process of . [3] . which is the output of goods and services which have . [4] ., i.e. the power to satisfy human wants. It is possible to define three ways in which this satisfaction is provided. Firstly, there is the process of turning raw materials into finished goods. This is known as the utility of . [5] . Secondly, there is the distribution of the goods from the factory to the shop. This is known as the utility of . [6] . Thirdly, there is the holding of the goods by the shopkeeper until such time as the consumer wants to buy them. This is known as the utility of . [7] . Because man's income is limited he is unable to buy all the goods and services he desires. He must exercise the power of . [8] . In order to increase the level of production by operating more efficiently the range of activities which a man carries out is limited. This process is known as . [9] . This process creates a situation of . [10] . because no man produces all that he needs. In order to widen the range of goods available to consumers a system of . [11] . has been developed.

utility	time	interdependence	form
scarcity	wealth	choice	exchange
production	specialisation	place	

2

THE ECONOMIC PROBLEM AND ECONOMIC SYSTEMS

1. Which is the best of the following statements about the Economic Problem?
   - (a) It is the problem of how to obtain the greatest income
   - (b) It is the problem of how to make the best use of things that are scarce
   - (c) It is a problem of how to get the money to buy all the things we want
   - (d) It is a problem of how to get things more cheaply than other people

2. *True/False?*
   - (a) Only economic goods can have a price
   - (b) Goods have a price only when there is an effective demand for them
   - (c) If goods are very scarce they cannot be economic goods
   - (d) Only useful goods are economic goods

3. Which of the following are true statements?
   - (i) The basic economic problem is one of choice
   - (ii) Choice is necessary because our resources are scarce
   - (iii) Resources are scarce because our wants are limited
   - (iv) The basic economic problem is the same for all economies
   - (a) all of them   (b) all but iii   (c) all but iv   (d) ii only

4. Which of the following is *not* an economic problem?
   - (a) Choosing between buying a record or going to the cinema
   - (b) Deciding how much of one's income to save
   - (c) Praying for more rain and less sun on the crops
   - (d) Deciding whether to work overtime or to take more leisure

5. Which one of the following is a *positive* economic decision?
   (a) To discourage smoking by raising the tax on cigarettes
   (b) To redistribute income in order to promote greater social equality
   (c) To raise prices in order to increase profits
   (d) To call for more Special Deposits in order to reduce the money supply

6. Different societies have evolved different methods of tackling the economic problem but while their methods are different their ultimate aim is the same. That aim is:
   (a) to make their country richer than all other countries
   (b) to make the best possible use of their available resources
   (c) to achieve the highest possible growth rate
   (d) to provide their consumers with the widest possible range of consumer goods and services

7. In a free enterprise economy what will be produced will ultimately depend on:
   (a) the success of a firm's advertising campaign
   (b) what is in the best interests of the country
   (c) the way in which consumers decide to spend their incomes
   (d) the independent decisions of producers

8. In a planned economy what will be produced will depend much more (than in a free enterprise economy) on:
   (a) the decisions of the relevant government department
   (b) the best interests of the individuals in the country
   (c) the need to help other countries
   (d) people producing directly to satisfy their own wants

9. In Britain our economic system is usually described as:
   (a) free enterprise   (b) planned
   (c) mixed   (d) underdeveloped

10. Which of the following distinguishes the planned economy from the free enterprise economy?
    (a) Choice plays a bigger part in consumer decisions
    (b) The profit motive is more evident in the productive system
    (c) The economic interests of the state are usually put before the economic interests of the individual
    (d) It enables a much larger output per head to be produced

11. In a mixed economy:
    (a) all economic decisions are made by the government and all non-economic decisions by individuals
    (b) all heavy industry is run by the government and all other economic enterprises by individuals
    (c) all social service activities are run by the government and all economic enterprises by individuals
    (d) some of the more essential economic activities are controlled by the government and the others are the responsibility of private individuals

12. In a capitalist economy most capital is privately owned while in a planned economy it is owned by the state. It follows that:
    (I) capital will inevitably be used more efficiently in a capitalist economy because of the profit motive
    (II) the real cost of building a school will be less in the planned economy because the capital, provided by the state, does not involve the individual in opportunity cost decisions
    (a) I only is true   (c) both I and II are true statements
    (b) II only is true   (d) neither I nor II are true statements

13. Which of the following are concerned to find the optimum combination of factors to produce a given output?
    (i) A capitalist economy   (iii) A private enterprise firm
    (ii) A planned economy   (iv) A nationalised organisation
    (a) i and iii   (b) iii only
    (c) i, iii and iv   (d) all of them

14. In a free enterprise system the way that scarce resources are allocated is determined primarily by:
    (a) rationing the scarce resources so that they are fairly distributed
    (b) the operation of the price mechanism: we get what we can afford to buy
    (c) the operation of retailers who decide what they will let their customers have
    (d) the government, a department of which distributes goods throughout the country

3

POPULATION

1. The growth of population in a country depends upon:
    (i) the number of births in a given period
    (ii) the number of deaths in a given period
    (iii) the number of marriages in a given period
    (iv) the number of people who immigrate
    (v) the number of people who emigrate
    (vi) the number of people who move within the country
    (a) all of these factors   (b) i, ii, iv, v
    (c) all but vi   (d) i and ii only

2. Which of the following offer possible reasons for the population explosion in the late eighteenth and early nineteenth centuries?
    (i) Medical improvements
    (ii) Better housing
    (iii) Fertility drugs
    (iv) Better diet
    (v) More opportunities for employment
    (vi) Increased knowledge of contraception
    (a) all of these reasons   (b) i and iv only
    (c) i, ii, iv and v   (d) all but iii

3. In a pre-industrial country with both birth rate and death rate at a relatively high level which of the following is likely to be the most effective in bringing about an increase in total population?
    (a) A fall in death rate while birth rate remains the same
    (b) A rise in birth rate while death rate remains the same
    (c) A rise in the average age at marriage
    (d) An increase in the number of children born to each family

4. Why is the population at present static or perhaps even declining? Because:
   (i) people cannot afford to have children
   (ii) people want to enjoy a higher standard of living
   (iii) people have greater knowledge of contraception
   (iv) the average number of children born to each family is declining
   (a) for all of these reasons   (b) ii, iii and iv
   (c) iii and iv   (d) iv only

5. Why are some demographers concerned at the prospect of a declining population?
   (a) Because there will not be enough labour to maintain our present living standards
   (b) Because population will then fall below the optimum
   (c) Because it will mean an ageing population and a smaller proportion of working age
   (d) Because a declining population means the end of our society

6. What is the ideal size of population for this country?
   (a) About 50 million
   (b) A size which maintains national output
   (c) A size which enables the population to be evenly distributed regionally
   (d) It is not possible to say for there are too many considerations to be borne in mind

7. What is the optimum population level? That level of population which:
   (a) maximises national output
   (b) maximises output per head
   (c) minimises the proportion not working
   (d) it is not possible to say

8. *True/False?*
   (i) Immigration has only recently become a problem for the British economy
   (ii) The net inflow of immigrants each year usually exceeds 50,000 people
   (iii) Migration can seriously affect the age and sex distribution of the population
   (iv) The population of the major cities of Britain has declined in the last ten years

9. Some demographers argue that we are heading for another Malthusian crisis. What do they mean?

   (a) Growth of population will outstrip the growth of the supply of food
   (b) Output will actually decrease because of the law of diminishing returns
   (c) The population will increase beyond its optimum
   (d) Pressure on space will lead to conflict between nations

10. Which of the following are features of over-population?

    (i) Dangers of pollution
    (ii) Reduction in the amount of land per head
    (iii) Lower marginal physical product of labour
    (iv) Fall in availability of raw materials per head

    (a) all of them   (b) all but iii
    (c) ii and iv only   (d) ii, iii and iv

11. *True/False?*

    (i) The normal sex distribution, i.e. ratio of men to women, is 105 : 100
    (ii) The life expectancy of males is lower than that of females
    (iii) There is an excess of men over women in urban areas
    (iv) The dependent groups are expected to reach 50% of the total population by 1980

12. In attempting projections of future population size, which of the following factors would you expect to be most variable in the next ten years?

    (a) Number of women of child bearing age
    (b) Average age at marriage
    (c) Average family size
    (d) Changes in the rate of divorce and illegitimacy

13. Which of the following are likely to affect population growth?

    (i) Land use   (iii) Other resources
    (ii) Housing   (iv) Environmental considerations

    (a) all of them   (c) ii only
    (b) all but iv   (d) none of them

4

THE FACTORS OF PRODUCTION

1. Which of the following is *not* a factor of production?
   (a) Land   (b) Labour   (c) Money   (d) Capital
   (e) Enterprise

2. Match the following:
   (i) land   (a) wages
   (ii) labour   (b) profit
   (iii) capital   (c) rent
   (iv) enterprise   (d) interest

3. Which of the following characteristics applies to capital?
   (a) All the free gifts of nature which yield an income
   (b) A stock of assets to assist in future production
   (c) An asset with no cost of production
   (d) A factor which is fixed in supply

4. Which of the following statements about factors of production is true?
   (a) Each factor has its own peculiar characteristics and are therefore not in competition with other factors
   (b) Production is possible as long as three of the four factors are present
   (c) Factors are in competition with each other for employment
   (d) Factors are perfect substitutes for each other

5. Which important economics concept is illustrated by the following schedule?

Units of Land (acres)	Number employed (men)	Output of Potatoes (cwts)
5	3	50
5	4	60
5	5	68
5	6	70

    (a) Law of Diminishing Marginal Utility
    (b) Law of Comparative Costs
    (c) Malthus's Law
    (d) Law of Diminishing Returns

6. Which of the following will affect the labour supply?

    (i) An improvement in educational standards
    (ii) A reduction in the average age at marriage
    (iii) A reduction in the age of majority
    (iv) A change in the sex ratio
    (v) The introduction of stricter immigration laws

    (a) i, ii and iii   (c) all but iii
    (b) iii, iv and v   (d) all of them

7. Which of the following could *not* be included in the category 'land' as a factor of production?

    (a) Fish in the sea
    (b) Coal in the ground
    (c) Heather for hillside grazing
    (d) Iron ore stock piles

8. Which of the following are functions of the factor 'enterprise'?

    (i) To decide how all the factors should be combined in production
    (ii) To take the risk of production
    (iii) To supply the physical effort in production
    (iv) To maximise profits

    (a) i only   (b) ii only   (c) all but iv   (d) all but iii

9. The income of a man who solely owns and runs his own shop and has no other source will in effect be made up of:
    (a) some profit, some wages, some interest and some rent
    (b) some profit, some wages and some rent
    (c) some profit and some wages
    (d) profit only

10. The least cost combination of factors for any given level of production occurs where:
    (a) the prices of the factors are proportional to their marginal products
    (b) the average products of the factors are proportional to their prices
    (c) the opportunity cost ratios of the two factors are lowest
    (d) the lowest amount is spent on the factors

11. Five hundred tons of cement can be produced by using the following combinations of men and machines each week:

	Men	Machines
(a)	2	10
(b)	5	8
(c)	10	6
(d)	16	4

If the total cost of operating each machine is £200 per week and if the men earn £35 per week, what will be the least cost combination?

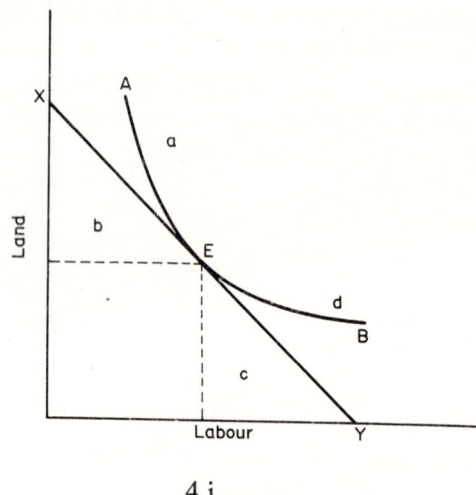

4.i

12. The diagram shows the optimum combination of factors when AB is an equi-product curve for various combinations of the factors, and XY shows the amounts of the two factors which could be employed for a given expenditure.

    If the rent of land was to increase while labour costs remained the same, where would the new optimum be placed on the diagram?

    Would it move towards: (a), (b), (c) or (d)?

13. Which of the following factors contribute to immobility of labour in this country?
    (i) Lack of knowledge of the labour market
    (ii) Government restrictions on the movement of labour
    (iii) Trade union restrictions on entry into certain jobs
    (iv) Modern specialisation limits the range of new jobs which can be taken up
    (v) There are no retraining facilities for those who wish to change jobs

    (a) i, iii, iv   (b) i, iv, v   (c) all but ii   (d) all of them

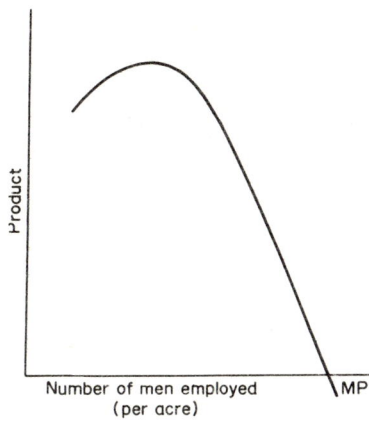

4.ii

14. Which of the following statements is best illustrated by the diagram?
    (a) The satisfaction obtained from the consumption of each extra unit of a good diminishes as more units are consumed
    (b) As price increases, the quality which will be produced increases
    (c) As the units of a variable factor are increased, while the amount of other factors employed remains the same, the additions to total output will diminish
    (d) The increase in specialisation made possible by an increase in the number of men employed brings about economies of sale

15. When the firm achieves optimum factor combination, all but *one* of the following is true. Which one is *not* true?
    (a) The firm must always be maximising its profits
    (b) The firm is producing a given output at lowest unit cost
    (c) The firm is making the best possible use of its factors in those circumstances
    (d) The line denoting the firm's total outlay is tangential to the highest possible equi-product curve for that given outlay

5

CONSUMER DEMAND

1. What is the object of all consumers in the way they spend their income?
   - (a) To buy the most goods and services possible
   - (b) To maximise the value of their purchase
   - (c) To maximise their utility
   - (d) To overcome the law of diminishing returns

2. What is the economic problem which faces all consumers?
   - (a) How to maximise their profits
   - (b) How to make the best allocation of their limited income
   - (c) How to reduce their opportunity cost
   - (d) How to increase their marginal utility

   Questions 3, 4 and 5 refer to the following schedule.

   Schedule of a consumer's demand for ice cream

Point	Number of ice creams consumed	Marginal Utility of ice cream in money terms	Price of ice creams
(a)	1	14p	5p
(b)	2	12p	5p
(c)	3	9p	5p
(d)	4	5p	5p
(e)	5	0p	5p

3. At what point will the consumer be in equilibrium with his purchases?

4. At what point is the consumer surplus greatest?

16

5. Which of the following is illustrated by the schedule?
    (i) The Law of Diminishing Marginal Utility
    (ii) Common Equilibrium in the purchase of a single commodity
    (iii) Equilibrium occurs where MU = Quantity Consumed
    (iv) The Opportunity Cost Principle
    (a) all of them   (c) all but iii
    (b) i and ii   (d) none of them

6. *True/False?*
    (i) A consumer is in equilibrium with all his purchases when there is no extra utility to be gained by rearranging them
    (ii) A consumer is in equilibrium when he allocates his income according to the principle $\frac{MU}{p}$ of good A = $\frac{MU}{p}$ of good B = $\frac{MU}{p}$ of good C, etc.

    (iii) A consumer is in equilibrium when he is unable to increase his satisfaction by spending more money.
    (iv) A consumer is in equilibrium if the spending of more money would yield only a diminishing marginal rate of satisfaction
    (v) The consumer will be in equilibrium when he has no wish to change the amounts of purchases he has made unless there is some change in the circumstances affecting his choice

7. Which of the following statements is compatible with the state of consumer equilibrium?
    (a) The consumer will buy as much as he can of the cheaper goods
    (b) The consumer will continue to alter his purchases until there is no extra (utility) satisfaction to be gained by doing so
    (c) If both incomes and the prices of all the goods he purchases are exactly doubled the consumer will double his purchases of goods in order to remain in equilibrium
    (d) The consumer will buy those goods which have the highest total utility

8. The real value of a commodity to a consumer is:
    (a) the total utility he obtains from it
    (b) the amount he pays for it
    (c) the amount of other things he has to give up to get it
    (d) its cost in relation to the consumer's income

9. The consumer's objective is to allocate his limited income in such a way as to:
    (a) buy the most goods and services
    (b) have the best effect on the British economy
    (c) obtain those goods and services which have the most quality
    (d) obtain those goods and services which give him the most utility

10. Which of the following would cause the consumer to alter his purchases in order to restore his equilibrium?
    (i) A change in his income
    (ii) A change in the price of the goods he buys
    (iii) A change in his preferences
    (iv) A change in the preferences of other consumers
    (v) A change in the marginal utility of one of the goods he purchases
    (vi) A change in the opportunity cost of one of the goods he purchases

    (a) none of them   (c) ii, iv, v and vi
    (b) all of them   (d) all but iv

11. The Paradox of Value is concerned with why it is that water, without which we cannot go on living, commands only a low price, while diamonds, which have little but decorative value, command a very high price. Which of the following gives the best explanation of the higher price of diamonds?
    (a) The marginal utility of diamonds is greater than the total utility of water
    (b) The total utility of diamonds is greater than the marginal utility of water
    (c) The marginal utility of diamonds is greater than the marginal utility of water
    (d) The total utility of diamonds is greater than the total utility of water

12. In which one of the following cases does the principle of Opportunity Cost not apply?
    (a) When a consumer alters his purchases in order to increase the utility he obtains
    (b) An increase in his income enables him to buy some more of each commodity
    (c) Because of the law of diminishing marginal utility he obtains less increase in total utility when he buys another unit of the good
    (d) A change in prices causes a shift along an indifference curve

13. An indifference map is a diagram showing:
    (a) how a consumer finds a way to increase his wealth
    (b) how a consumer allocates his limited income between various combinations of two commodities
    (c) the equi-marginal returns concept
    (d) the satisfaction obtained from various combinations of two commodities increases towards the origin

Questions 14-17 are based on diagram 5.i

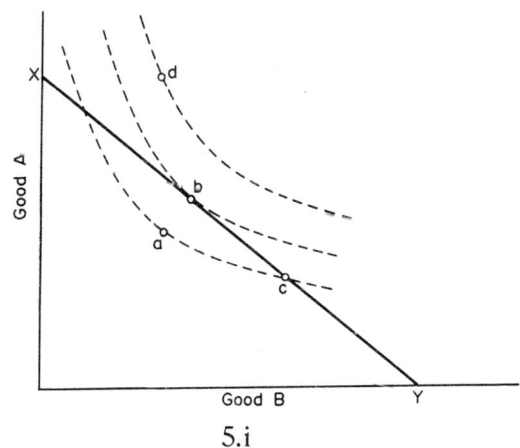

5.i

14. At which point in the circumstances illustrated in the diagram will the consumer be in equilibrium with his purchases?

15. Without the limitations imposed by the income line XY, at which of the given points would the consumer obtain greatest utility?

16. If there were a rise in the Price of Good B, other things remaining the same, towards which of the given points would the equilibrium move?

17. If there were an increase in the consumer's income, other things remaining the same, towards which point would the equilibrium move?

18. *True/False?*

   (i) An indifference curve is an equi-utility contour
   (ii) The marginal rate of substitutability of two commodities can be shown by an indifference curve
   (iii) If the law of diminishing marginal utility did not apply, the indifference curve would not necessarily slope downwards to the right
   (iv) The consumer is in equilibrium where one indifference curve is tangential to the next one

6

MARKET DEMAND

1. The market demand for a commodity consists of:
   - (a) all demand which can be found in the market place
   - (b) the sum of all individual consumers' demands
   - (c) all that could be bought with consumers' incomes
   - (d) the demand forthcoming at a particular price in the market

2. The market demand curve will *normally* slope:
   - (a) vertically
   - (b) downwards to the left
   - (c) downwards to the right
   - (d) horizontally

3. What is the usual effect of an increase in price on the demand for that good?
   - (a) It remains the same
   - (b) It falls
   - (c) It rises
   - (d) An infinite increase

4. Which of the following factors directly affect the market demand for a commodity?
   - (i) The price of the good
   - (ii) The price of complementary goods
   - (iii) The price of competitive goods
   - (iv) Consumers' incomes
   - (v) Consumers' tastes
   - (vi) The supply of the commodity
   - (a) all of them
   - (b) all but ii and v
   - (c) only i
   - (d) all but vi

5. The effect of a change in the price of one good on the demand for another good is best measured by:
   (a) the Opportunity Cost fraction
   (b) the marginal rate of substitutability
   (c) the coefficient of cross-elasticity
   (d) the Law of Diminishing Marginal Utility

6. What will be the effect of a fall in consumers' incomes on the market demand for a commodity, other things remaining the same?
   (a) A change in income is irrelevant to market demand
   (b) There will be a rise in demand
   (c) There will be a fall in demand
   (d) There will be no change in demand

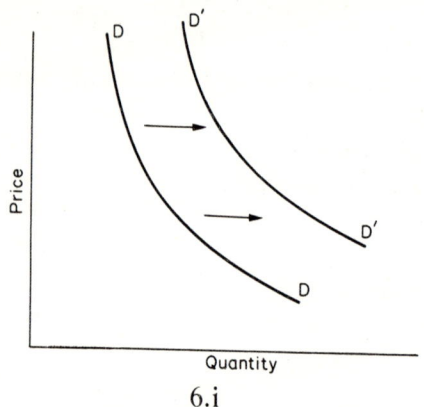

6.i

7. Which of the following could explain the above diagram of changing demand conditions?
   (a) A fall in the price of a complementary good
   (b) A fall in the price of a competitive good
   (c) A rise in the price of an inferior good
   (d) A fall in consumers' incomes

8. Which of the following offers the best definition of price elasticity of demand?
   (a) The ease with which producers can alter their output in response to a change in price
   (b) The response of consumers' tastes to a change in price
   (c) The rate of response of demand to a change in supply
   (d) The rate of response of demand to a change in price

9. In which of the following circumstances could demand be described as inelastic?
   (a) An increase in price brings about a fall in demand
   (b) An increase in price brings about an increase in consumer spending
   (c) A fall in price brings about an increase in revenue
   (d) A fall in price brings about no change in the amount spent by consumers

10. *True/False?*
    (i) If price elasticity of demand for a commodity is less than unity a fall in price would bring about a less than proportionate fall in the quantity purchased
    (ii) The demand curves for all commodities which have unitary elastic demand will be rectangular hyperbolas
    (iii) The demand curves for all commodities which have inelastic demand will be vertical straight lines
    (iv) The demand for luxuries must always be elastic

Schedule of demand for frozen chickens

Price per lb		Quantity demanded (000s)
20p	W	12
21p	X	9
22p	Y	7
23p	Z	6.5
24p		6.3

11. Using the above schedule, say which of the following statements are true.
    True/False?
    (i) Demand is elastic for all prices on the schedule
    (ii) The coefficient of elasticity is highest at W
    (iii) Demand is inelastic at Z
    (iv) The total spent by consumers increases as price rises at Y
    (v) Elasticity of demand is unitary at X

12. Income elasticity of demand can be defined as:
    (a) the effect of a rise in income on price
    (b) the rate of response of demand to a change in income
    (c) the rate of response of income to a change in demand
    (d) the change in tastes resulting from a change in income

13. If the average income of consumers rises from £30 to £35 per week and the demand for sherry increases as a result from 60,000 to 65,000 bottles, we can say that the income elasticity of demand for sherry is:

    (a) unitary
    (b) inelastic
    (c) elastic
    (d) not known, because there is not enough information

	Price of Butter per lb	Quantity of Butter m lb	Price of Bread per loaf	Quantity of Bread m loaves
(a)	55p	23	10p	60
(b)	50p	30	11p	50
(c)	45p	35	12p	40
(d)	40p	42	13p	25
	35p	50	14p	10

14. In the above schedule, at what point is the cross-elasticity of demand for butter and bread nearest to 10?

15. If a rise in consumers' incomes brings about a fall in demand for margarine we would say that margarine was:

    (a) income elastic
    (b) a Giffen good
    (c) an inferior good
    (d) price inelastic

7

THE EQUILIBRIUM OF THE FIRM

1. *True/False?*
   (a) The total costs of the firm are made up only of payments to the factors of production
   (b) The total costs of the firm are the sum of fixed costs and variable costs
   (c) Total costs divided by units of output gives average variable costs
   (d) In the long run there are no variable costs

2. Which one of the following is a fixed cost to the firm?
   (a) The cost of raw materials
   (b) Overtime payments to workers
   (c) The rent of the factory
   (d) Fuel for the production process

3. Which one of the following is a variable cost to the firm?
   (a) The managing director's basic salary
   (b) The productivity bonus paid to higher management
   (c) The lighting for the factory
   (d) That part of the depreciation of a machine which is due to age

Diagram 7.i applies to Questions 4 and 5

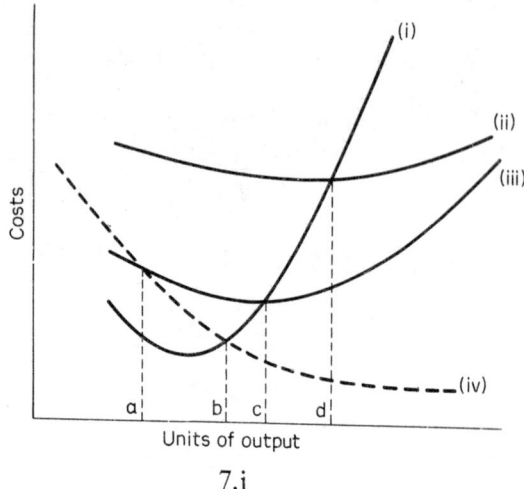

7.i

(a) = Average Total Cost Curve
(b) = Average Variable Cost Curve
(c) = Average Fixed Cost Curve
(d) = Marginal Cost Curve

4. Match the curves with the letters above:
   (i) =   (iii) =
   (ii) =   (iv) =

5. On the diagram, which is the optimum point of production:
   a, b, c, d?

6. Which of the following reasons help to explain why the
   average total cost curve falls at first?
   (i) Possibilities of specialisation by factors produce
       economies of scale
   (ii) The law of diminishing returns
   (iii) Fuller use of capacity reduces the effect of the element of
       fixed costs
   (iv) Variable cost per unit declines until the optimum is
       reached
       (a) all of them   (b) ii and iii   (c) i and iii
       (d) none of them

7. Which of the following help to explain why the average total cost curve rises after the optimum?

   (i) After a point the scale of production produces problems which existing management cannot cope with efficiently
   (ii) As the firm approaches capacity bottlenecks and shortages occur
   (iii) The law of diminishing returns
   (iv) Diseconomies of scale begin to apply

   (a) all of them   (b) all but iii   (c) all but iv
   (d) just i and ii

8. Which of the following offers the best definition of Marginal Cost?

   (a) The last unit produced
   (b) The increase in total costs resulting from an increase in output by one unit
   (c) The amount which the firm receives for one more unit of production
   (d) The total cost divided by output

9. 'The point of lowest unit cost of production' is a definition of:

   (a) equilibrium   (c) economy of scale
   (b) optimum   (d) profit maximisation

10. Which of the following is *not* a condition of the perfect market?

    (a) A large number of buyers and sellers operating in the market
    (b) The firm must be a 'price-maker'
    (c) There must be freedom of entry into the market
    (d) There must be perfect knowledge of the market by consumers

11. Under perfect competition which of the following statements are true?

    (i) The Price curve will be a horizontal straight line
    (ii) Price will be equal to average revenue
    (iii) Price will be equal to marginal revenue
    (iv) The equilibrium of the marginal firm will occur where Marginal Cost, Average Cost, Marginal Revenue, Price, and Average Revenue are all equal

    (a) none of these is true   (c) all but iv are true
    (b) i and iii are true   (d) all are true

Questions 12-14 are based on diagram 7.ii

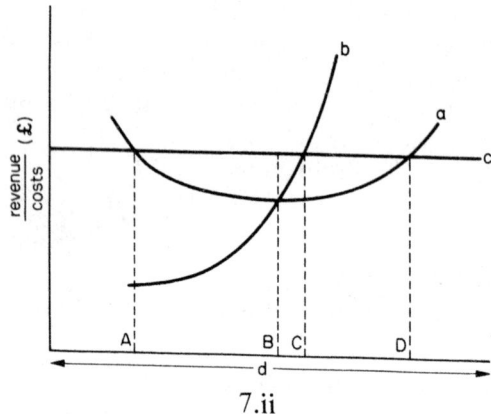

7.ii

12. Match the following (with reference to diagram 7.ii) with a, b, c, or d:

   (i) Marginal Cost of the firm is shown on the diagram by:
   (ii) Average Total Cost of the firm is shown on the diagram by:
   (iii) the Output of the firm is shown on the diagram by:
   (iv) the Marginal Revenue of the firm is shown on the diagram by:

13. If the firm aims to maximise its profits will it produce at the output on the diagram labelled A, B, C, or D?

14. At the equilibrium level of output the firm will make:
   (a) only normal profits because the firm is operating under perfect competition
   (b) excess profits because it is a super-marginal firm
   (c) excess profits shown by the difference between costs at the optimum and revenue at the price line
   (d) only enough to cover costs in the short run, and in the long run it would go out of business

Questions 15-17 are based on the following schedule for a firm producing colour television sets.

	Output	AT.C (£)	M.C. (£)	Price (£)
	20	190		170
(a)			140	
	30	173		170
(b)			140	
	40	165		170
(c)			160	
	50	164		170
(d)			170	
	60	165		170
(e)			180	
	70	166		170

15. At what output is the firm producing at the optimum?

16. At what output is the firm in equilibrium?

17. From the schedule we can see that the colour television firm is:
   (a) an oligopolist
   (b) a monopolist
   (c) a marginal firm in an imperfect market
   (d) a super-marginal firm in a perfect market

18. Which of the following conditions would you expect to find in a market where there is monopolistic competition?
   (i) A homogeneous product
   (ii) Advertising
   (iii) A price curve which slopes downward to the right
   (iv) No entry into the market
   (v) Perfect knowledge of the market

   (a) all of them   (b) all but i and v   (c) ii and iii only
   (d) none of them

19. The main difference between the oligopolistic market and that of monopolistic competition is that under oligopoly:
   (a) a few sellers dominate the market
   (b) there is little competition because of market sharing agreements
   (c) the product is not homogeneous
   (d) entry into the market is not possible

20. A discriminating monopolist attempts to:
    (a) produce at optimum in each of the markets in which he operates
    (b) maximise his profits in each of the markets in which he operates
    (c) bring about product differentiation
    (d) prevent all entry into the market

Questions 21-26 are based on diagram 7.iii

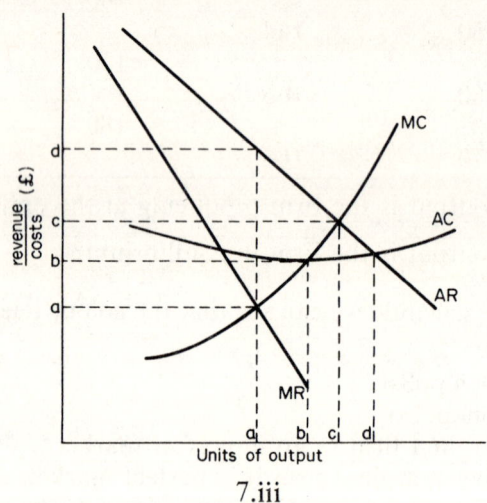

7.iii

21. The diagram depicts the equilibrium of:
    (a) a super-marginal firm in the imperfect market
    (b) a marginal firm in the imperfect market
    (c) a super-marginal firm in the perfect market
    (d) a marginal firm in the perfect market

22. Which is true on the diagram: (a) MR = Price, or (b) AR = Price?

23. At what level of output would the firm be in equilibrium?

24. What is the optimum level of output of the firm?

25. What price should the firm charge to maximise its profits?

8

SUPPLY

1. Market Supply consists of:
   (a) the total amount which could be offered for sale by all the firms in the market
   (b) the amount produced by all firms producing at equilibrium output
   (c) the amount produced by all firms producing at optimum output
   (d) the amount produced by all firms which yields super-normal profits

2. Which of the following statements about Supply is true?
   (a) The normal supply curve slopes downwards to the right
   (b) Supply always increases the longer the time period
   (c) The quantity offered for sale increases as price falls
   (d) The value of a given supply depends upon the consumers' effective demand for it

3. Which of the following statements is correct?
   The Market Supply curve will slope upwards to the right:
   (a) when there are speculative conditions in the market
   (b) when all suppliers must accept the price ruling in the market
   (c) when suppliers respond to rising prices by increasing their output
   (d) when suppliers have no time to respond to price changes

4. Which of the following statements is *incorrect?*

   (a) The steepness of the supply gives some indication of elasticity of supply curve
   (b) The supply curve will slope most steeply when supply is inelastic
   (c) The supply curve will slope more steeply in the long period
   (d) Shortage of raw materials can cause the supply curve to slope more steeply

5. What conclusion about market supply can be drawn from the following diagram showing the cost curves of the firm in two time periods?

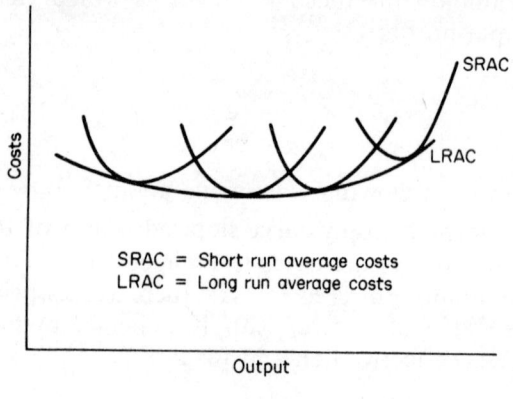

SRAC = Short run average costs
LRAC = Long run average costs

8.i

   (i) Only at the long run optimum will both short run and long run optimums coincide
   (ii) Market supply will be more elastic in the short run
   (iii) Economics of Scale operate more effectively in the long run
   (iv) The Law of Diminishing Returns takes effect more quickly in the short run

   (a) all of them   (c) all but ii
   (b) ii, iii and iv   (d) none of them

Questions 6 and 7 are based on the following schedule:

Supply Schedule for Alarm Clocks

Price	Quantity offered for Sale (000s)
£2.00	10
£2.50	11
£3.00	12.5
£3.50	15
£4.00	20

(a), (b), (c), (d) markers are placed between the price rows:
- (a) between £2.00 and £2.50
- (b) between £2.50 and £3.00
- (c) between £3.00 and £3.50
- (d) between £3.50 and £4.00

6. At what point is supply most elastic?

7. At what point is elasticity of supply nearest to unity?

8. Which of the following factors is most likely to have brought about the change illustrated in the diagram?

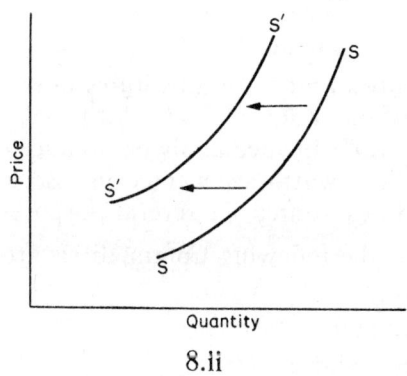

8.ii

(a) A fall in consumer incomes
(b) A shortage of labour
(c) A merger between two firms operating in the market
(d) A new invention reducing unit costs of production

9. The supply curve of the firm and the market supply curve will necessarily coincide under:

(a) perfect competition
(b) monopolistic competition
(c) oligopoly
(d) pure monopoly

10. Which of the following is likely to have the most inelastic supply?
    (a) Natural rubber
    (b) Potatoes
    (c) Plastic buckets
    (d) Antiques

11. *True/False?*
    (i) The Market Period allows no time for suppliers to respond to a change in price
    (ii) The Short Period allows time for variable factors to be increased or decreased
    (iii) In the Long Period there are no fixed factors
    (iv) It is possible for the Long Period Supply Curve to slope downwards to the right though eventually it must rise

12. Match the following with the definitions below:
    (i) joint supply
    (ii) joint demand
    (iii) composite supply
    (iv) composite demand

    (a) commodities which are substitutes in meeting the satisfaction of one want
    (b) commodities which can only be produced in association
    (c) commodities which are wanted in association
    (d) commodities wanted for several purposes

13. Say which of the following Commodities are examples of:
    (i) joint supply
    (ii) joint demand
    (iii) composite supply
    (iv) composite demand

    (a) electricity and gas
    (b) butter and margarine
    (c) gas and coke
    (d) bacon and eggs

14. Why do entrepreneurs offer a given quantity for sale at a given price?
    (a) To maximise their profits
    (b) To satisfy people's wants
    (c) To help to overcome the economic problem
    (d) To maximise their revenue

9

PRICE

1. Which is the main function of the price mechanism?
   (a) To allocate scarce resources among competing wants
   (b) To indicate the real value of things
   (c) To enable producers to make a profit
   (d) To limit consumer demand

2. What is equilibrium price?
   (a) The price at which demand and supply are equal
   (b) The price at which producers maximise their profits
   (c) The price at which consumers maximise their utility
   (d) The price at which production is at the optimum

Demand and Supply Schedules for Hot Cross Buns

	Price	Quantity Demanded (000s)	Quantity Supplied (000s)
(a)	2p	10	3
(b)	2½p	8	4
(c)	3p	7	5
(d)	3½p	6	6
	4p	5	8

3. Referring to the schedule above, at what price will there be equilibrium in the market?

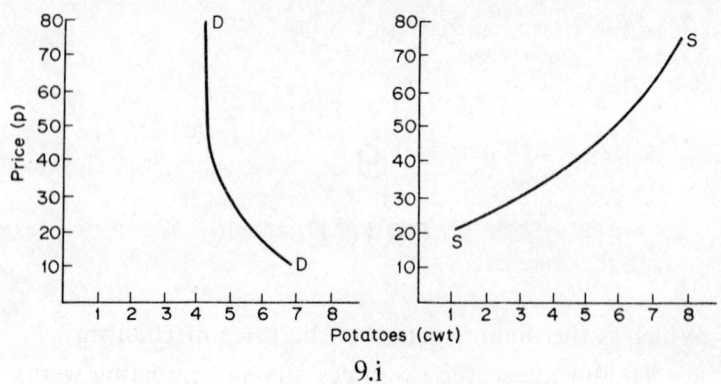

Potatoes (cwt)

9.i

4. In diagram 9.i, at what level of price will there be equilibrium in the market for potatoes:

   (a) between 10p and 30p   (c) 40-50p
   (b) 30-40p   (d) above 50p

5. If there is an increase in demand, supply conditions remaining the same:

   (a) both Price and Quantity sold will fall
   (b) both Price and Quantity sold will rise
   (c) Price will rise but the change in Quantity sold cannot be
       determined without more information
   (d) without more information no comment can be made
       about Price or Quantity

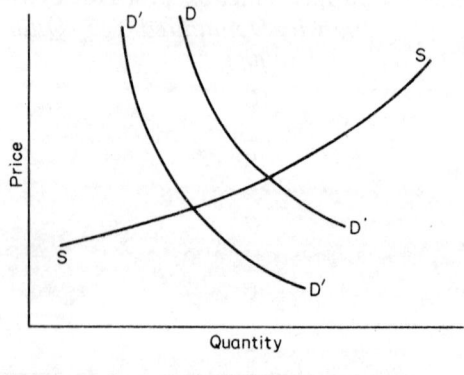

9.ii

6. Given the change in demand conditions shown in diagram 9.ii, what conclusion can be drawn?
    (a) Both Price and Quantity sold will fall
    (b) Both Price and Quantity sold will rise
    (c) Price will rise but the change in Quantity sold cannot be determined without more information
    (d) Without more information no conclusion can be drawn about Price or Quantity

7. The government imposes a further 10% indirect tax on records. What will be the effect on the price of records?
    (a) It will rise by 10%
    (b) It will not rise at all
    (c) The price rise will depend on the relative elasticities of demand and supply
    (d) There is insufficient information to draw any conclusion

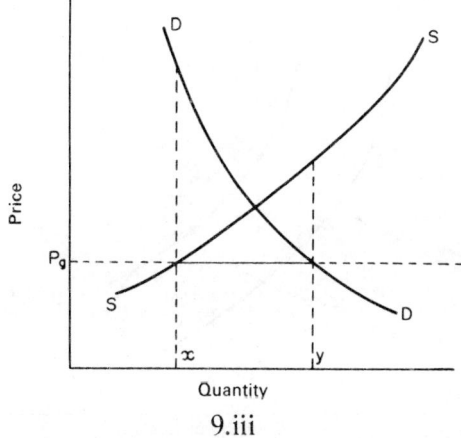

9.iii

8. The government establishes price control of eggs at P_g (see diagram 9.iii). If it wishes to maintain this price there must be:
    (i) rationing to reduce demand to X
    (ii) subsidies to persuade producers to increase their output from X to Y
    (a) either (i) or (ii) is needed
    (b) both (i) and (ii) are needed
    (c) there is no need for (i) or (ii)
    (d) there is not enough information to draw any conclusions

9. Egg Farmers asked the Price Commission to approve an increase in the price of eggs in order to restore profit levels. The Commission argued that profits could be restored by reducing prices to increase sales. The question of which side is right in the argument depends upon:

   (a) whether there are economies of scale in egg production
   (b) the relative elasticities of demand and supply of eggs
   (c) whether egg production is already at the optimum
   (d) the nature of the market for eggs

10. If the government imposed a heavy tax on tea, what would be the effect on the price and quantity of milk sold?

    (a) Both price and quantity would increase
    (b) Both price and quantity would decrease
    (c) It depends on whether tea and milk are complementary or competitive goods
    (d) None, since the market for milk is quite independent of that for tea

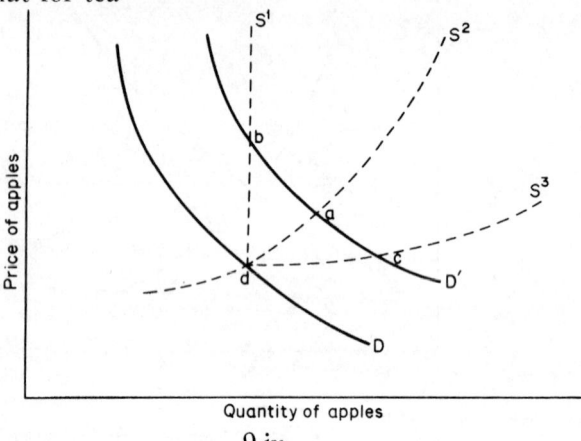

Quantity of apples

9.iv

11. Diagram 9.iv shows:

    (a) a disequilibrium position with three possible equilibria resulting from an increase in demand
    (b) the aggregation of the supply of three firms towards a single equilibrium at 'd'
    (c) the effect of an increase in demand on equilibrium price and quantity depends upon the time which suppliers have to respond
    (d) a change in supply conditions brings about a considerable increase in demand from D to D'

12. Match the following with the letters in the diagram 9.iv:

    (i) market period equilibrium
    (ii) short period equilibrium
    (iii) long period equilibrium

13. Recently 5,000 silver goblets were sold to commemorate the millennium of a well-known cathedral. Many requests for goblets were unsatisfied. Which of the following conclusions can be drawn?

    (a) The market for the goblets would have borne a higher price
    (b) The price of the goblets should have been lower
    (c) *Effective* demand was equal to supply at the price charged
    (d) The silversmiths must have been subsidised

14. *True/False?*

    (a) If the government interferes with the price mechanism there must be a maldistribution of scarce resources
    (b) Goods which have the highest prices have the highest value
    (c) The lower the combined coefficient of elasticity of demand and supply the higher the price
    (d) Where the combined coefficients exceed zero a fall in price must increase expenditure on the product

15. Statement I. An increase in demand will bring about a rise in price if other things remain the same

    Statement II. A rise in price will bring about a fall in demand if other things remain the same

    (a) both statements are true, and as a result there is no change in demand
    (b) only Statement I is true
    (c) only Statement II is true
    (d) both statements are true, but they refer to different market situations and so II does not follow from I

10

THE STRUCTURE OF INDUSTRY

1. As economists we should aim for that structure of industry which:
   (a) reduces the firms operating in that industry to a minimum
   (b) allows firms to operate at their optimum
   (c) makes the largest profits possible in that industry
   (d) maximises the numbers of firms operating in the market

2. Which of the following statements is *necessarily* true?
    (i) The larger the number of firms the greater the competition
    (ii) The more competition the more efficient the industry
    (iii) The stronger the monopoly the greater the profits it will make
    (iv Concentrated industries tend to be monopolies

   (a) none of them   (c) all but iv
   (b) ii and iii   (d) all of them

3. Which of the following offers the best definition of an industry? A group of firms:
   (a) producing similar products by similar methods
   (b) using similar methods to produce differing products
   (c) producing products which are in competition
   (d) using the same raw materials

4. Statement   I. The structure of industry depends upon the nature of the product
   Statement   II. The structure of industry depends upon the nature of the market
   Statement III. The degree of independence or integration between firms in an industry is an important determinant of its structure

   (a) Each of the three statements is true and compatible with the others
   (b) All the statements are true but could not all apply simultaneously
   (c) Statement I and Statement II are not compatible
   (d) Statement III is not compatible with Statements I and II

5. *True/False?*
    (i) The best use of resources occurs when all firms in an industry are producing at their optimum
    (ii) All economies of scale produce reductions in unit costs of production
    (iii) Because economies of scale result from growth of production, it always pays a firm to grow
    (iv) A firm can enjoy economies without any increase in its scale of production

6. (a) farming   (b) retail trade   (c) furniture making
    (d) rubber tyres
    In which of the above industries would you expect the optimum size of the firm to be largest?

7. In which of the above industries would you expect the optimum size of the firm to be the smallest?

8. Match the following:
    (i) an industry dominated by a single firm
    (ii) a firm producing products in several different industries
    (iii) an industry dominated by a small number of firms
    (iv) a horizontal or vertical grouping of firms exercising monopoly powers
    (a) a trust   (c) a monopolist
    (b) an oligopolist   (d) a conglomerate

9. Match the following:
    (i) business owned and controlled by a restricted number of shareholders
    (ii) business controlled by the government
    (iii) business owned and controlled by shareholders
    (iv) business owned and controlled by members
    (a) a co-operative society   (c) a public company
    (b) a public enterprise   (d) a private company

10. They result from: (i) concentration of industry in an area
    (ii) the splitting off of specialist processes to be operated by a specialist firm
    (iii) the development of a pool of trained labour
    (iv) the opening up of improved communications to the area

The above all apply to: (a) internal economies of scale
    (b) external economies of scale
    (c) optimum production
    (d) technical economies of scale

Questions 11-14 refer to the following types of economies of scale:

(a) technical
(b) managerial
(c) marketing
(d) financial

11. All the responses i-iv describe how *one* of the types of economies of scale is gained. To which of the economies do the responses apply?

An increase in the scale of production:

(i) gives the firms greater profits to plough back
(ii) makes the firm better known, which attracts investors
(iii) enables the firm to cut the cost of raising capital
(iv) specialisation enables the firm to make better use of working capital

12. To which of the economies do these responses apply? They

(i) may be on the buying or selling side of the business
(ii) result from buying materials or parts in bulk
(iii) result from lorries being loaded more fully
(iv) result from sales staff being more fully employed

13. To which of the economies do these responses apply? They

(i) are not confined to manufacturing industries
(ii) result from greater specialisation
(iii) result from linking of processes
(iv) impose no limit on the scale of production

14. To which of the economies do these responses apply? They
    (i) soon turn to diseconomies if the firm becomes too large
    (ii) arise from functional specialisation
    (iii) arise from delegation of detail
    (iv) can be increased by specialist equipment

15. Which of the following, resulting from an increase in the scale of output, helps to reduce the risk involved in production?
    (i) Diversification of markets
    (ii) Diversification of products
    (iii) Diversification of sources of raw materials
    (iv) Grouping of risks
    (v) More specialised management

    (a) all of them   (c) all but iv and v
    (b) all but v   (d) ii and iii only

16. Match the following methods by which firms grow:
    (i) combination between firms operating similar processes
    (ii) combination between firms producing different products
    (iii) combination between the firm and suppliers of raw materials or essential parts
    (iv) combination between the firm and the distributors of its products
    (v) combination between the firm and firms operating ancillary processes

    (a) vertical integration   (c) diagonal integration
    (b) horizontal integration   (d) conglomeration

17. Which of the following is probably *not* a reason why firms grow?
    (a) To increase financial control
    (b) To increase profits
    (c) To increase the share of the market
    (d) As a defensive reaction to the growth of other firms

18. Which of the following is *not* a method by which firms finance their operations?
    The issue of:
    (a) equities   (c) preference shares
    (b) unit trust shares   (d) debentures

19. Match 18 (a), (b), (c) and (d) with the following definitions:
    (i) securities issued in return for a long period loan usually secured by a mortgage
    (ii) securities which give their holders a prior claim to payment of dividends
    (iii) ordinary shares which normally entitle the holder to vote on company affairs
    (iv) shares in a block holding of a range of stock spread over many different securities

20. *True/False?*
    (i) The market concentration ratio is the extent to which a market is dominated by a single firm
    (ii) The proportion of Britain's G.N.P. produced by Britain's top 100 companies is increasing
    (iii) The optimum level of production in some industries is larger than the markets for that country's output alone can bear
    (iv) A Nationalised Enterprise cannot produce at the optimum because it is too large

21. If it is generally true that larger firms are more efficient, why are some mergers against the public interest?
    (a) Because mergers inevitably mean that the price will be higher and the quality supplied lower
    (b) Because mergers inevitably mean a reduction in competition and therefore in efficiency
    (c) Because the monopoly profits earned by the merged firm are unacceptable
    (d) Because the merger gives the firm more than one-quarter of the market

22. Why does the Monopolies Commission find that some mergers are against the public interest? Because:
    (i) the merger would give the firm more than one-third of the market share
    (ii) of the monopoly profits earned by the firm with the reduction in competition
    (iii) the reduction in competition would produce a decline in the service to customers
    (iv) mergers always produce a rise in price and a decline in quantity produced

    (a) all of them   (c) ii and iii only
    (b) all but iv   (d) ii only

23. The Resale Prices Act of 1964 allowed five gateways for exemption from the ban on R.P.M. Which of those shown below is *not* a 'gateway'?
    (a) That profits would be reduced in the long run
    (b) That prices would be increased in the long run
    (c) That after-sales service would be substantially reduced
    (d) That the number of retail outlets would be substantially reduced

24. Which of the following was the second hurdle which all firms had to clear before the ban on R.P.M. would be lifted for them?
    (a) The benefits from R.P.M. must exceed the benefits from its abolition
    (b) The profits resulting from R.P.M. must be reduced
    (c) The competition in foreign markets must be stepped up
    (d) Retailers must be seen to benefit from R.P.M.

25. The 1965 Monopolies and Mergers Act made it possible:
    (i) to deal with mergers more quickly and effectively
    (ii) to investigate restrictive practices in the service industries
    (iii) to impose conditions on acquisitions of other firms
    (iv) to investigate mergers when the value of assets exceeded £50 million

    (a) all of them   (c) i only
    (b) all but iv   (d) none of them

26. *True/False?*
    (i) 'Fighting Companies' are set up to apply pressure on a well established monopolist
    (ii) A 'Damages Agreement' was compensation paid to a retailer for a price cut by a monopolist
    (iii) Resale Price Maintenance applies to goods in the second-hand market
    (iv) A discriminating monopolist charges different prices in different markets

11

THE LOCATION OF INDUSTRY

1. The tendency for firms to set up in an area is said to depend on: (a) natural (b) acquired (c) cumulative (d) comparative advantages.

   (i) To which of the above does the existence of a skilled labour force belong?
   (ii) To which of the above does the momentum from sympathetic movements of labour belong?
   (iii) To which of the above does the existence of a navigable river belong?
   (iv) To which of the above does the advantage of the firm in competing successfully for factors of production within the area belong?

2. It is possible to apply the law of comparative costs to the location of industry. Which of the following offers the best definition of this law?

   (a) An area should specialise in the production of those goods in which it has the greatest advantage
   (b) Even if an area can produce goods more efficiently than its neighbours, it may be worth allowing its neighbours to produce those goods so that the factors of the area can be concentrated on more valuable production
   (c) Two areas can produce a greater amount from the same amount of factors if each concentrates on the goods it can produce best
   (d) It pays area I to allow area II to produce those goods in which its disadvantage is least marked, so that area I can concentrate on the production of those goods in which its advantage is most marked

3. Which of the following have *not* been areas of marked industrial concentration?

   (i) North-West England   (iv) The Scottish Highlands
   (ii) The Midlands   (v) East Anglia
   (iii) South Wales   (vi) London and the
                                      South-East

   (a) none of them   (c) i and iv
   (b) iv, v and vi   (d) iv and v

4. Which of the above are development areas?

   (a) i, iii and iv   (c) all of them
   (b) all but vi   (d) none of them

5. Which of the following has had the highest average rate of
   unemployment in the last ten years?

   (a) South Wales   (c) North-West England
   (b) Scottish Highlands   (d) North-East England

6. Which of the following statements about industrial concen-
   trations in an area seems to carry most weight?

   (a) Industrial concentration should be encouraged because
       it provides employment
   (b) Industrial concentration should be discouraged because
       over-dependence on an industry increases the risk of
       pockets of heavy unemployment
   (c) Industrial concentration reduces transport costs and so
       increases efficiency
   (d) Industrial concentration should be discouraged because
       it spoils the environment

7. There has been a reduction in the concentration of industry
   since the war because of:

   (i) the development of sources of power which are less
       heavily locational
   (ii) the movement of labour from the industrial areas
   (iii) the regional development policies carried out by the
       government

   (a) all three are correct   (c) i and iii are correct
   (b) only i is correct   (d) ii and iii are correct

8. Government Regional Planning has been directed towards:
   (i) reducing the level of unemployment
   (ii) raising the level of investment
   (iii) creating a suitable infra-structure
   (iv) increasing the Growth Rate
   (v) spreading industry evenly between the regions

   (a) all of them   (c) all but iii and iv
   (b) all but i and ii   (d) all but v

9. In attempting to achieve their objectives for the regions, which of the following measures have governments employed *in the last ten years?*
   They have
   (i) established industrial training boards
   (ii) moved labour from the development areas
   (iii) given 40% investment grants
   (iv) prohibited all industrial development over 1,000 sq. ft. in Midlands and South-East
   (v) given Regional Employment Premiums

   (a) all of these   (c) i, iii and v
   (b) all but ii and iii   (d) all but iv

10. Why should the Government determine the regional multiplier before finally deciding on its regional policy?
    (a) So that the number of firms likely to be attracted to the area can be decided
    (b) So that the 'labour mobility factor' can be worked out
    (c) So that the effect of a given investment injection on the income of the area can be ascertained
    (d) So that the modification of the infra-structure of the area will become clear

11. *True/False?*
    (i) Despite the expenditure of huge sums by the Government the Development Areas still have rates of unemployment above the average for the country
    (ii) All industrial building has been controlled by I.D.C.s, which are Investment Documents of Credit
    (iii) The effectiveness of government policy can be criticised because many of the industries attracted to the regions were capital rather than labour intensive
    (iv) S.E.T. was more effective than the R.E.P. in reducing the level of unemployment in the regions

12. Which of these statements about the effect on regional policies of Britain's entry into the E.E.C. is true?
    (a) Britain will have to cease making grants to the development areas under the terms of the Treaty of Rome
    (b) Britain will have to pay out far more to the development areas of the other E.E.C. members than she will receive for her development areas
    (c) Britain will receive more for her development areas than she has to pay out to help the development areas of the other countries
    (d) Britain's regional policies will be unaffected

13. The 'Location Quotient' is:
    (a) the factor by which a given investment injection must be multiplied to ascertain the expected growth of income in the area
    (b) a measure of the precise degree of specialisation in the area
    (c) the deviation of the distribution of workers in various areas from the distribution over the whole country
    (d) the deviation of government investment in development areas from the average distribution over the whole country

14. Match the following:
    (i) cotton   (a) dispersed
    (ii) shipbuilding   (b) moderate localisation
    (iii) iron and steel   (c) fairly high localisation
    (iv) retail trade   (d) high localisation

15. Match the occupation with the approximate percentage distribution of the total working force:
    (i) agriculture   (a) 50%
    (ii) construction   (b) 33%
    (iii) other manufacturing   (c) 3%
    (iv) services   (d) 7%

12
MONEY

1. Which of the following *cannot* be said to be a function of
   money? It:
   (a) provides utility
   (b) is a unit of account
   (c) is a store of value
   (d) is a medium of exchange

2. Which of the following is the most essential characteristic of
   money?
   (a) Durability
   (b) Acceptability
   (c) Portability
   (d) Divisibility

3. *True/False?*
   (i) If there were no money, exchange would require 'a
       double coincidence of wants'
   (ii) The most important thing about money is its intrinsic
        value
   (iii) Money is created by the issue of notes and coins
   (iv) Money is anything that is generally acceptable in pay-
        ment of debts

4. *True/False?*
   (i) We should all be richer if tomorrow the Government
       declared the value of money to be doubled
   (ii) The real value of money is what it will buy in terms of
        goods and services
   (iii) We should all be richer if tomorrow the Government
         doubled the quantity of money
   (iv) We should all be richer if tomorrow the Government
        doubled our incomes

5. In Britain the basic money supply (Ml) consists of:
   (i) coins
   (ii) notes
   (iii) current accounts
   (iv) gold
   (a) all of them (b) all but iv (c) just i and ii (d) the basic money supply includes several other items which do not appear in the list

6. This basic money supply in January 1975 amounted to roughly:
   (a) £1,500 million
   (b) £15,000 million
   (c) £150,000 million
   (d) £150 million

7. Why do people *normally* want to hold money?
   (i) So that they can take advantage of opportunities to use it to make more money
   (ii) In case some misfortune should require them to spend it
   (iii) So that they can buy goods and services with it
   (iv) Because it has intrinsic value to them
   (a) for all these reasons
   (b) for all but iv
   (c) for either i, ii or iii, but never all three together
   (d) for i and iii

8. Match i-iv above with the terms below:
   (a) hoarding motive
   (b) precautionary motive
   (c) speculative motive
   (d) transactions motive

9. What do you understand by liquidity preference?
   (a) The desire to put money away for a rainy day
   (b) The desire to hold money rather than other assets
   (c) The desire to hold assets in a form which can easily be converted into cash
   (d) The desire not to run an overdraft at the bank

10. Which of the following can affect the supply of money?
    (i) Government monetary policy
    (ii) The rate of interest
    (iii) Credit creation by the banks
    (iv) The definition of legal tender
    (a) all of them (b) i and ii (c) i, ii and iii (d) ii only

11. Banks can create money by:
    (a) opening up deposits for borrowers
    (b) taking in more money from depositors
    (c) writing more cheques
    (d) printing more notes

12. (a) 1½%   (b) 12½%   (c) 28%   (d) 30%
    (i) What is the current cash ratio which the banks are required to maintain?
    (ii) What is the current eligible reserve assets ratio which the banks are required to maintain?

13. If the bank's eligible reserve assets are increased by £100 it can increase its lending by:
    (a) £300   (b) £800   (c) £7,500   (d) £101.50

14. Which of the following measures can the Bank of England use to reduce the money supply?
    (i) Increased taxation
    (ii) Freeze private customers' accounts at the Bank
    (iii) Special deposits
    (iv) Last resort lending rate
    (v) Ceilings on lending
    (vi) Open market operations
    (a) iii, iv, vi   (b) i, v, vi   (c) all but i and ii   (d) all of them

15. Why is a rise in interest rates expected to reduce the money supply?
    (a) Because it encourages saving
    (b) Because it encourages investment
    (c) Because it discourages borrowing
    (d) Because it diverts money into other channels

13

BANKS AND OTHER FINANCIAL INSTITUTIONS

1. Which is the 'odd man out' of the following list?
    (a) Commercial banks
    (b) Joint Stock banks
    (c) Clearing banks
    (d) Merchant banks

2. Which of the following are functions of a Clearing Bank?
    (i) The acceptance of commercial bills
    (ii) The issue of securities
    (iii) The safekeeping of deposits
    (iv) Making loans to customers
    (v) Making profits for shareholders

    (a) all but i and ii   (c) all but v
    (b) iii and iv only   (d) all of them

3. Which of the following items appear on the assets side of a bank's balance sheet?
    (i) Current accounts
    (ii) Deposit accounts
    (iii) Deposits by overseas residents
    (iv) Balances with other U.K. banks
    (v) Bills discounted

    (a) all of them   (c) iv and v
    (b) i, ii and iii   (d) all but iii

4. Which of the following financial institutions undertakes *all* the functions outlined below?
    (i) Authorised dealing in foreign exchange
    (ii) Acceptance of commercial bills
    (iii) Issue of securities
    (iv) International lending and borrowing of surplus funds
    (v) Advising on company finance

    (a) discount houses   (c) merchant banks
    (b) overseas banks   (d) commercial banks

5. In 1972 the government introduced new measures to encourage competition and credit control. Which of the following changes were included in those new measures?
    (i) Credit control arrangements to be extended to financial institutions other than banks
    (ii) An increase in the proportion of commercial bills accepted as 'eligible'
    (iii) The abolition of special deposits
    (iv) A change from a liquidity ratio of 28% to a reserve assets ratio of 12½%
    (v) A reduction in the cash ratio from 8% to 1½%
    (a) all of them   (c) i, ii and iii
    (b) i, iv and v   (d) none of them

6. From the items listed below pick out those which are regarded as 'eligible' for reserve purposes:
    (i) cash in the banks' tills
    (ii) U.K. Treasury Bills
    (iii) all money at call in the London money market
    (iv) all money at call in the interbank market
    (v) five-year government bonds
    (v) a proportion of local authority bills
    (a) all of them   (c) all but iv and v
    (b) all but i and ii   (d) ii, iii and vi only

7. *True/False?*
    (i) The Big Four clearing banks still operate cartel arrangements on interest rates
    (ii) Bank rate was abolished in 1972
    (iii) Open Market Operations is concerned with the Bank of England buying industrial securities at the Stock Exchange
    (iv) Special Deposits, being the frozen assets of the Clearing Banks, earn no interest

8. Which of the following measures would you recommend to a Chancellor of the Exchequer who wanted to increase the supply of money in the economy?
   (a) Instruct the Issue Department of the Bank of England to have more notes printed
   (b) Reduce the sale of Treasury Bills and government bonds to the discount houses
   (c) Raise the rate at which the Bank of England would lend in the last resort
   (d) Redefine eligible reserve assets

9. During 1972 the Bank of England was not holding Special Deposits from the Clearing Banks. This was because:
   (a) the economic problems, which Special Deposits were intended to solve, did not exist in 1972
   (b) in the new deal for competition and credit control there. was no place for Special Deposits
   (c) the rate of interest paid on these deposits was not attractive enough to the banks
   (d) the authorities were relying on other measures to deal with the economic problems

10. In attempting to reduce the supply of money the Bank of England could use all but *one* of the following measures:
    (a) an increase in the last resort lending rate
    (b) a reduction in the availability of eligible reserve assets
    (c) an increase in the Clearing Banks' deposit rates
    (d) funding

11. Which of the following is *not* a function of the Bank of England?
    (a) To make profits for its shareholders
    (b) To manage the foreign exchange rates
    (c) To manage the National Debt
    (d) To accept deposits from private customers

12. *True/False?*

    (i) The commercial banks keep their reserves at the Bank of England

    (ii) Foreign banks with offices in London have larger deposits than the London Clearing Banks

    (iii) Negotiable Certificates of Deposit enable the banks to get higher interest rates on short term deposits

    (iv) The banks' holdings of Treasury Bills exceed their holdings of commercial bills

13. The rate of discount on commercial bills is higher than that on Treasury Bills because:

    (a) the risk of handling commercial bills is greater

    (b) the sums involved are much greater

    (c) because they are usually for a much longer period

    (d) the discount houses operate a cartel arrangement which drives the rate up

14. Although they are widening the range of their activities, one of the following items is *not* normally dealt in by discount houses:

    (a) government securities

    (b) industrial securities

    (c) local authority securities

    (d) commercial bills

15. Which of the institutions listed below operate in the Euro dollar market?

    (i) British overseas banks

    (ii) American banks

    (iii) Merchant banks

    (iv) Local authority brokers

    (v) Finance houses

    (a) ii only   (c) all but iv and v

    (b) i and ii   (d) all of them

16. What is the main reason for the issue of Treasury Bills?

    (a) To provide the government with funds for its day to day operations

    (b) To provide the Treasury with funds for long term investments

    (c) To keep the discount houses in operation

    (d) To 'mop up' the surplus funds of the commercial banks

17. Match the following:

    (i) London Gold Market   (a) BOLSA
    (ii) London Stock Exchange (b) Rothschilds
    (iii) Finance houses   (c) Mullens
    (iv) British overseas bank (d) North Central Wagon

18. Match the following:

    (i) Discount house   (a) Prudential
    (ii) Accepting house   (b) Gillett Bros
    (iii) Assurance company (c) Kleinwort Benson
    (iv) Unit trust   (d) Slater Walker

19. In which of the institutions listed below would you expect to find all the following?

    (i) Jobbers (ii) Brokers (iii) Waiters (iv) Stags (v) Bulls
    (vi) Bears

    (a) Foreign Exchange   (c) the Commodity Markets
        Market   (d) the Stock Exchange
    (b) the Gold Market

20. What is the job of a broker at the Stock Exchange?

    (i) To speculate on industrial stocks
    (ii) To buy and sell stocks on behalf of their customers
    (iii) To buy and sell stocks on their own behalf
    (iv) To make a turn by quoting different buying and selling prices

    (a) all of them   (c) all but iv
    (b) all but i   (d) ii only

21. A person who takes a bullish view of the stock market:

    (a) expects prices to fall
    (b) expects prices to rise
    (c) hastens to sell his shares
    (d) is not a speculator but an investor

22. The American banks operating in London:

    (a) are only there to take part in the Euro-currency business
    (b) compete with the Clearing Banks in all aspects of their business
    (c) hold larger total deposits than the Clearing Banks
    (d) do not have to make Special Deposits with the Bank of England

23. Discount houses in their 1973 operations increased most rapidly their holdings of:
    (a) British Government Stocks
    (b) Treasury Bills
    (c) commercial bills
    (d) sterling certificates of deposit

24. Which of the following statements about accepting houses is true?
    (a) They usually hold more than £10 million in coins, notes and balances with the Bank of England
    (b) They do not have to make Special Deposits with the Bank of England
    (c) Acceptances are their biggest single item of business
    (d) They lend money at call to the discount houses

25. *True/False?*
    (i) Accepting houses usually keep more than 14% of their assets in eligible reserve items
    (ii) Money at call is the largest single item in the total reserve assets of all financial institutions
    (iii) Building societies are not subject to the same reserve requirement as banks
    (iv) Finance houses usually keep reserve assets of less than 11%

14

PUBLIC FINANCE

1. Why do we expect the government to provide a wide range of social services instead of leaving it to private enterprise to provide them?

   (i) To avoid wasteful duplication of services
   (ii) The supply of these services should not depend on the profit motive
   (iii) Only the government could afford to supply them
   (iv) Only the government has the power to subsidise them from taxation

   (a) all of them
   (b) all but iii
   (c) i and ii only
   (d) iv only

2. For which of the following reasons would you expect the government to increase its expenditure?

   (i) To increase the range of social services provided
   (ii) To raise the general level of employment
   (iii) To strengthen its defence policy
   (iv) To reduce a balance of payments deficit

   (a) i and iii only
   (b) i, ii and iii
   (c) all but ii
   (d) all but iv

3. Taxation can be used for a number of purposes. Which of the following describe uses of taxation in this country?

   (i) To raise revenue for the government
   (ii) To regulate the level of economic activity
   (iii) To confiscate all inherited wealth
   (iv) To bring about greater equality of incomes
   (v) To encourage firms to plough back profits

   (a) i, ii and iii
   (b) iii, iv and v
   (c) all but iii
   (d) all of them

4. Which of the following is *not* likely to be an objective of the government in reforming the taxation system?

   (a) To make the system more regressive
   (b) To simplify the system
   (c) To reduce the proportion of each pound tax revenue going in costs of collection
   (d) To bring our tax system more into line with those of E.E.C. countries

5. Just prior to a General Election a government decides to increase its expenditure without raising the level of taxes. Which of the following would be likely to occur as a result?

   (a) An increased deficit on the balance of payments
   (b) An increased rate of inflation
   (c) An increase in the National Debt
   (d) We should need more information before accepting any of the above conclusions

6. Under what circumstances would an increase in taxes lead to a more than proportionate decrease in consumer spending?

   (a) The increased taxes reduced the spending by lower income groups, which reduced the income and spending of others, and so on
   (b) When the elasticity of the goods taxed was greater than unity
   (c) When the tax was progressive in the higher income brackets
   (d) When increased taxes make saving more attractive

7. Which of the following is *not* a fiscal measure which might be used by the government to affect the level of employment?

   (a) A change in the rate of V.A.T.
   (b) An increase in the level of tax allowances
   (c) The use of the regulator
   (d) Restrictions on hire-purchase

8. *True/False?*

   (i) Taxes on expenditure are a debit item in National Income accounting
   (ii) Britain's basic rate of V.A.T. is lower than that of most other countries in the E.E.C.
   (iii) V.A.T. is a direct tax
   (iv) V.A.T. was expected to produce more revenue than the old purchase tax (1972-73)

9. Match the following items of government expenditure with the nearest estimated total (1974-75):   *in £'000 million*

   (i) defence and external relations   (a) 3.5
   (ii) social services   (b) 2.7
   (iii) environmental services   (c) 4.2
   (iv) commerce, industry and nationalised
       industries   (d) 11.3

Incomes (£)	Amount Paid in Tax (£)
10,000	3,000
8,000	1,300
6,000	900
4,000	650
2,000	300

10. How would you describe the tax system indicated in the table above?

   (a) Progressive   (c) Regressive
   (b) Proportional   (d) Marginal

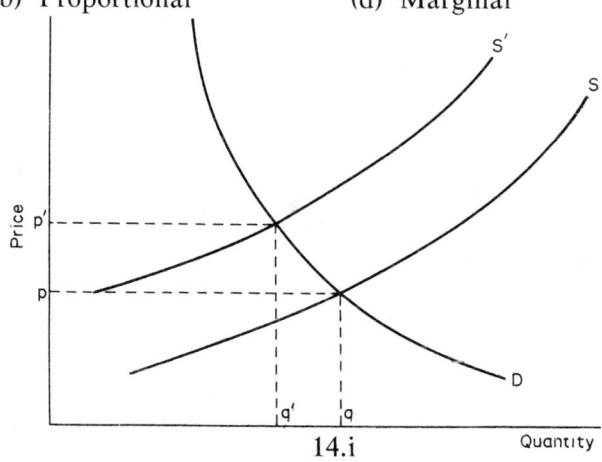

14.i

11. The above diagram could be used to illustrate:

   (a) the effect of an increase in income tax on the equilibrium price of the good
   (b) the effect of an increase in indirect tax on the equilibrium price of the good
   (c) the fall in demand resulting from a subsidy on the supply of a good
   (d) the effect of a decrease in V.A.T. on the equilibrium price of a good

12. In the list below which is the odd-one-out?
    (a) Budget surplus
    (b) Increased taxation
    (c) Reduced government expenditure
    (d) Demand spending on consumer goods

13. Which of the following is an indirect tax?
    (a) Surtax   (c) Estate Duty
    (b) Income Tax   (d) Excise Duty

The following questions apply to changes in the tax system in 1972-3.

14. Match the following:
    (i) Income Tax   (a) A tax to redirect employment abolished
    (ii) Purchase Tax   (b) A direct tax simplified
    (iii) Value Added Tax   (c) An indirect tax abolished
    (iv) S.E.T.   (d) An indirect tax introduced

15. Which of the following statements about V.A.T. are true?
    (i) The introduction of V.A.T. is a considerable simplification of the tax system
    (ii) The introduction of V.A.T. means a considerable reduction in the tax collected
    (iii) V.A.T. is charged at two rates, standard and exempt
    (iv) V.A.T. is a tax paid by a trader on value added
    (v) V.A.T. is in effect a tax on consumers' expenditure

    (a) All of them   (c) i, ii, iii and v
    (b) iii, iv and v   (d) Some combination not
                                      mentioned in a, b, or c

16. The government arranged for a system of Unified Personal Tax to be introduced. What is meant by this?
    (a) One rate of tax will apply to all persons regardless of the level of their income
    (b) One rate of tax will apply to all persons' incomes up to £5,000
    (c) It is a progressive rate of tax at all levels of income
    (d) One rate of tax will apply to all unearned incomes up to £5,000

15

NATIONAL INCOME
AND
THE THEORY OF EMPLOYMENT

1. What is the National Income? Which of the following offer a possible definition?
   (i) The income received by the country in international trade
   (ii) The total amount of money in the country
   (iii) The income of all persons, firms and institutions in the country
   (iv) The total value of all goods and services produced in the accounting period
   (a) iii and iv
   (b) iii only
   (c) iv only
   (d) all of them

2. What are transfer payments?
   (a) Payments from one person to another
   (b) Allowances made by a man to his wife
   (c) The payment needed to persuade a man to change his job
   (d) Payments other than those made for productive sources

3. How does international trade affect National Income accounting?
   (a) It has no effect because National Income accounting is concerned with a closed economy
   (b) The amount earned by exports is added and the amount paid for imports subtracted
   (c) The amount earned by exports is subtracted and the amount paid for imports is added
   (d) Because total payments abroad must equal total receipts from abroad, it has no effect on National Income accounting

4. What are the main debit items in the National Income accounts?

   (i) Exports
   (ii) Imports
   (iii) Taxes
   (iv) Subsidies
   (v) Stock appreciation

   (a) all of them
   (b) i, iii and v

   (c) ii and iv
   (d) ii, iii and v

5. The net National Income of the U.K. in 1973-74 was approximately

   (a)   £6,000m.
   (b)   £25,000m.

   (c)   £60,000m.
   (d)   £100,000m.

6. Transfer Incomes are not included in the National Income accounts because
   (a) they are payments to persons living abroad
   (b) there is no way of calculating them
   (c) their inclusion would result in 'double counting'
   (d) they represent payment for economic activity generating income

7. The following table omits plus and minus signs and gives no guide where the totals should be drawn. Which of the possible answers is the correct one for the National Income?

	£m.
Income from employment and self-employment	30,000
Gross trading profits of companies	7,000
Gross trading surpluses of public corporations and other public enterprises	1,500
Rent	2,200
Total domestic income	
Stock appreciation	700
Gross domestic income	
Net income from abroad	500
Gross national product	
Capital consumption	3,500
National Income	

   In £'000m.
   (a) 32.0
   (b) 38.4

   (c) 44.0
   (d) 45.4

8. *True/False?*

    (i) The National Income is the sum of all payments to the factors of production
    (ii) The largest single item of expenditure generating G.N.P. is government spending
    (iii) By adding together total consumption and total investment we get the total national income
    (iv) Wages has the largest share of the distribution of the national income

9. In calculating the National Income government services are included:

    (a) at cost price
    (b) only if they are not transfer payments
    (c) only if they are financed by borrowing
    (d) only if they show a profit

10. Which of the following should *not* be included in the net National Income?

    (a) Rents from a castle in Spain
    (b) A field marshal's salary
    (c) The dole received by an unemployed engineer
    (d) The fees received by a schoolmaster for extra tuition

11. Which of the following offer a possible definition of growth?

    (i) An increase in the National Income in money terms
    (ii) A rise in the average standard of living of the population
    (iii) An increase in the real G.N.P. *per capita*
    (iv) A rise in the productive potential of the nation

    (a) all of them   (c) iii and iv
    (b) all but i   (d) ii only

12. What advantage is most likely to result from economic growth?

    (a) Everyone will be better off
    (b) There will be more National Product to be shared among the population
    (c) Growth will produce material benefits with no extra real costs
    (d) People's money incomes will increase

13. Which *one* of the following methods is most likely to lead to an increased growth rate?
    (a) A greater share of G.N.P. going to investment
    (b) A rise in interest rates
    (c) An increase in wages and profits
    (d) An increase in consumer demand

14. The level of employment in the country is determined most fundamentally by:
    (a) the decisions of employers
    (b) the level of aggregate demand
    (c) the decisions of workers
    (d) the level of wages

15. Aggregate Supply could be defined as:
    (a) the total cost of the output made by the fully employed community
    (b) the amount which employers must receive to make a given volume of employment worth while
    (c) the rising cost associated with growing employment
    (d) the expected receipts from the employment of a given number of men

16. The equilibrium level of employment in the economy will occur:
    (a) at full employment level
    (b) where the gap between aggregate demand and aggregate supply is covered by the budget surplus
    (c) where employers' business expectations match what they will have to pay to employ a given number of workers
    (d) the highest possible G.N.P. is being produced

17. Aggregate Demand is made up of:
      (i) consumers' expenditure
     (ii) businessmen's expenditure
    (iii) government expenditure
     (iv) savings
    (a) all of them   (c) i and ii
    (b) i only   (d) i, ii and iii

18. What determines *most fundamentally* the amount which people will spend out of their income?
    (a) Propensity to consume
    (b) Tastes
    (c) Taxation
    (d) The level of income

19. What is the marginal propensity to save?
    (a) The amount saved out of a given income
    (b) The amount saved out of a given increase in income
    (c) The average amount saved
    (d) The marginal amount saved

20. What is the marginal efficiency of capital?
    (a) The increase in output resulting from employing one more machine
    (b) What employers expect to receive from a given investment project
    (c) The reduction in cost resulting from the employment of one more machine
    (d) The net receipts resulting from capital investment

21. *True/False?*
    (i) Income flows because everyone's income is someone else's expenditure
    (ii) Income flows because everyone's expenditure is someone else's income
    (iii) Investment adds to the flow of income
    (iv) Saving adds to the flow of income

22. Match the definitions with the terms below:
    (i) the figure which indicates the total change which will occur in the level of income after a given change in expenditure has taken full effect
    (ii) the increase in investment demand which results from an increase in the level of consumption demand
    (a) the regulator   (c) the accelerator
    (b) the multiplier   (d) the deflator

23. Which of the following offers the best definition of the inflationary gap?
    (a) Government expenditure not covered by taxation
    (b) The difference between the total supply of money in one year and that of the next
    (c) The difference between the total supply of money and the total output of goods and services
    (d) The excess aggregate demand over aggregate supply at the full employment level

24. In an economy the marginal propensity to save is 1/5th. The total of households' incomes is increased by £500 million. How much extra will be spent in the first round of transactions?
    (a) £500m.   (c) £100m.
    (b) £400m.   (d) 0

25. $$k = \frac{1}{1 - \frac{\Delta c}{\Delta y}}$$ is the formula for:
    (a) marginal propensity to save
    (b) marginal propensity to consume
    (c) average propensity to consume
    (d) the multiplier

26. If the equilibrium level of income in an economy is £20,000m, and the marginal propensity to consume is 3/4, and the government decides to inject an extra £2,000m. into the economy, what will be the new equilibrium level of income?
    (a) £28,000m.   (c) £8,000m.
    (b) £22,500m.   (d) £2,500m.

16

INCOME DISTRIBUTION

1. Match the following:

   (i) wages   (a) land
   (ii) profit   (b) labour
   (iii) rent   (c) capital
   (iv) interest   (d) enterprise

2. Which of the following does *not* help to determine the elasticity of demand for labour?

   (a) The ease with which labour can be substituted for capital
   (b) The proportion of wages in total costs
   (c) The elasticity of demand for the product being produced
   (d) The ease with which extra men can be taken on

3. Which of the conditions below would cause the demand curve of the firm for labour to move to the left?

   (i) The prospect of prolonged strike action
   (ii) A fall in the price of a commodity for which demand is inelastic
   (iii) A wage rise
   (iv) A labour saving invention

   (a) all but iii   (c) iii and iv
   (b) i and iii only   (d) all of them

4. What is the main function of interest?

   (a) To reward the entrepreneur for his organisation
   (b) To compensate investors for giving up the present use of their capital
   (c) To distribute a company's profits among shareholders
   (d) To enable the government to obtain funds

5. Why is it unlikely that there will be a fall in the rent of land? Because:
   (a) land is always increasing in fertility
   (b) the free gifts of nature are becoming increasingly productive
   (c) land is fixed in supply while the demand for it is growing
   (d) land is the best medium for speculative activities

Questions 6-9 are based on diagram 16.i

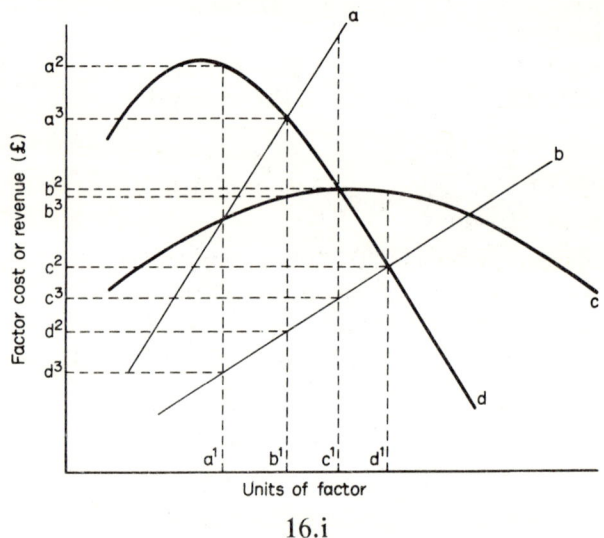

Units of factor

16.i

6. Match the curves on diagram 16.i with the following:
   (i) marginal factor cost
   (ii) average factor cost
   (iii) marginal revenue product
   (iv) average revenue product

7. In the circumstances indicated by the diagram above, what number of units of the factor would you recommend the firm to employ?

   a' b' c' or d'

8. What return will the factor receive from the entrepreneur in this market if employment is at the equilibrium level?

   a^2 b^2 c^2 or d^2

9. What return will the firm receive from that employment?

   a^3 b^3 c^3 or d^3

10. Match the following, which deal with the market for factors of production:

    (i) many buyers and many sellers   (a) monopsony
    (ii) one seller and many buyers   (b) competition
    (iii) one buyer and many sellers   (c) bilateral monopoly
    (iv) one buyer and one seller   (d) monopoly

11. If we assume that a firm operating in a competitive market for labour is unable to fix its wage rate unilaterally, and if we also assume that it wants to maximise its profits, which of the following statements would be true?

    (a) The firm will employ the number of workers which in the given production situation will produce the greatest possible output
    (b) The firm will continue to take on more workers until the addition to total costs resulting from employing one more worker is just equal to the addition to total revenue
    (c) The firm will employ the amount of labour which maximises the difference between marginal cost and marginal revenue for the marginal unit
    (d) The firm will get together with the trade union to fix the price of labour

12. Which one of the following is most likely to occur if trade unions force a wage settlement which at the existing level of output means that the marginal wage is above the marginal revenue productivity of the workers?

    (a) The higher wage rate will attract more men into employment in the firm
    (b) Output will be increased to meet the higher cost of labour
    (c) The firm will immediately go bankrupt
    (d) Firms will not replace workers who retire or move off to other jobs

13. Match the following:
    (i) economic rent   (iii) transfer earnings
    (ii) quasi rent   (iv) normal profits
    (a) The minimum payment necessary to keep a factor in its present employment
    (b) The minimum award necessary to persuade an entrepreneur to continue to undertake production
    (c) The surplus over and above the payment necessary to keep a factor in its present employment
    (d) The surplus arising from a short term inelasticity of supply

14. An important function of profit in a capitalist economy is to:
    (a) reward entrepreneurs for risk-taking and decision-making
    (b) provide income for shareholders
    (c) persuade people to save
    (d) provide capital for industry

15. An ice cream vendor could earn £25 a week driving a dust cart but he is prepared to continue in his present employment as long as he earns at least £23 a week. In fact over the years his earnings average out at £30 a week. Recently he has found a good 'pitch' in a newly built housing estate which has boosted his earnings to £40 per week. Soon, however, this boom will be over and his earnings will return to normal. What will be his:
    (i) normal economic rent
    (ii) quasi rent
    (iii) normal transfer earnings
    (iv) normal profits
    (a) £23   (b) £17   (c) £10   (d) £7

16. The law of variable proportions, sometimes known as the law of diminishing returns, states that as additional units of a variable factor are added to the fixed factors there will come a point beyond which the marginal product will begin to diminish. Which of the following statements does *not* follow from the law?

    (a) Given 'quantity produced' as the vertical axis and 'number of workers employed' as the horizontal axis, the marginal physical product curve will eventually slope downwards to the right

    (b) Because the marginal product of labour will eventually begin to diminish it will not be worthwhile the firm taking on more labour after that point is reached

    (c) The rate of increase in the total output of the firm resulting from successive additions of one more man, will eventually diminish, other things remaining the same

    (d) Unless the supply of the other factors can be increased in the same proportion, the rate of increase in the total output from additional men employed will eventually begin to diminish

17. In the case of the ice cream vendor in Question 15, his income will be:

    (a) all profit
    (b) some profit and some wages
    (c) some profit, some wages and some interest
    (d) some profit, some wages, some interest and some rent

17

INTERNATIONAL TRADE

Fill in the words missing from the paragraph, using the words and phrases printed below. Some words or phrases may be used more than once and some are distractors.

The theory of international trade is based on an extension of the principle of . [1] . A separate theory is required for international trade because unlike the theory of location we have to take into account such factors as:

(a) . [2] .   (b) . [3] .

(c) . [4] .   (d) . [5] .

A country must obviously import those goods which it is unable to . [6] . But it also pays the country to import those goods which other countries can . [7] . Even if the country produces all the things it needs cheaper than other countries could do, it may still be worthwhile buying some goods abroad so that it can concentrate its scarce factors on . [8] . goods. Two countries can produce a greater amount from the same amount of factors if each . [9] . on the things it can . [10] . The choice of these things depends upon the . [11] . available in that country. The goods produced therefore tend to reflect the relative abundance of these . [12] . China might be expected to produce goods which are . [13] . -intensive, and the United States those which are . [14] . intensive. The eventual nature of specialisation in international trade is determined by the law of . [15] . There are several advantages arising for a country following this principle, e.g.: (i) it should make possible a rise in its . [16] . (ii) it should make a . [17] . of goods available. Despite these advantages many countries choose to protect industries which have no comparative advantage. This may be because the industries are still in their . [18] . or because they have a vital . [19] . role to play. Protection enables import- . [20] . to take place. However protection inevitably raises the . [21] . of goods to the consumer.

balance of payments   trade barriers   infancy   absolute
substitution   produce cheaper   specialises
produce best   labour   comparative cost   price
more valuable   factors   capital   diminishing returns
produce itself   standard of living   wider range
currency problems   language barriers   strategic

1. *True/False?*

    (i) It is not possible for trade to take place between two countries, where one country can produce all things more cheaply than the other

    (ii) Because Free Trade makes goods available more cheaply to consumers it is impossible to justify protective measures

    (iii) Specialisation between countries makes it possible for those countries to produce more with a given amount of factors than they could otherwise have done

    (iv) The theory of comparative costs does not apply within a country

2. Which of the following reasons help to explain why trade is worthwhile?

    (i) Some countries produce goods more efficiently than others

    (ii) Countries are differently endowed by climate and other 'free gifts of nature'

    (iii) There are language and currency differences between countries

    (iv) The quantity and quality of the supply of factors differs between countries

    (a) all but iii   (c) i only

    (b) all of them   (d) i and iv

3. Below are listed three reasons for trade. Indicate which of the reasons offers a statement of comparative costs:

    (i) Two countries can produce a greater amount from the same factors if each specialises in the goods it can produce best

    (ii) If country A allows country B to specialise in the goods in which its disadvantage is least marked, while A specialises in those goods in which its advantage is most marked, a greater amount will be produced

    (iii) Even if a country can produce a commodity more cheaply than other countries, it may still pay to buy that commodity abroad so that its factors can be concentrated on the production of more valuable goods

    (a) all three reasons   (c) ii only

    (b) i only   (d) ii and iii

4. Why do countries adopt protective measures despite all the advantages arising from Free Trade?

    (i) To help to balance their payments
    (ii) To make their country richer (i.e. build up gold reserves)
    (iii) To build up infant industries
    (iv) To shelter high cost industries in order to maintain employment

    (a) for all of these reasons   (c) i and iii
    (b) i only   (d) i, iii and iv

5. An improvement in the terms of trade of a country indicates that:

    (a) imports have become cheaper in relation to exports
    (b) the quantity of imports has increased in relation to the quantity of exports
    (c) exports have become cheaper in relation to imports
    (d) the quantity of exports has increased in relation to imports

6. An improvement in the terms of trade must lead to an improvement in the balance of payments:

    (a) if demand for imports is inelastic
    (b) if demand for exports is inelastic
    (c) if demand for imports and exports is unitary
    (d) if demand for both imports and exports is inelastic

7. Which is the largest export item by value in U.K. trade?

    (a) Machinery
    (b) Chemicals
    (c) Coal
    (d) Textiles

8. Which is the largest import group by value in U.K. trade?

    (a) Foodstuffs
    (b) Raw materials
    (c) Fuel
    (d) Manufactures

9. In which area has U.K. trade grown most rapidly in the 1970s?
   (a) Sterling Area
   (b) North America
   (c) Western Europe
   (d) The rest of the world

10. Which of the policy measures outlined below would be likely to help to correct a deficit on the current account of the balance of payments at least in the short run?
    (i) A reduction in the tourist allowance
    (ii) The introduction of import licences
    (iii) An 'export drive'
    (iv) Subsidies on exported goods
(a) i only	(c) all but ii
(b) i and iii	(d) all of them

11. 'Britain's balance of payments is in fundamental disequilibrium'. Which of the following best elucidates this statement?
    (a) Britain is consuming more than she is producing
    (b) The pound sterling is fluctuating wildly in value
    (c) The imbalance between visible imports and exports is too great to be met by the surplus on invisibles and currency flow items
    (d) All the policies attempted by the government in recent years to deal with balance of payments problems have been unsuccessful

12. Which of the following measures adopted or permitted by the government would *not* produce expenditure-switching?
    (a) 1964—import surcharge
    (b) 1967—devaluation
    (c) 1968—import deposit scheme
    (d) 1970—rising interest rates

13. What is the difference between expenditure-switching and expenditure-dampening policies?

    (a) The former aims at switching expenditure from one overseas market to another, while the latter aims to reduce demand in the foreign market

    (b) The former is used when there is a balance of payments surplus and the latter when there is deficit

    (c) The former is accomplished by changing the price of foreign goods in relation to domestic goods while the latter relies on a reduction in aggregate expenditure

    (d) 'Dampening' policies are aimed at countries with whom we have a deficit, while 'switching' is concerned with moving trade from those countries to others where we have a surplus

14. *True/False?*

    (i) Britain's balance of payments position has worsened each year since the devaluation of 1967

    (ii) The main effect of adopting a flexible exchange rate policy has been to increase the country's gold and foreign currency reserves

    (iii) The period 1970-73 saw a net inflow of capital from abroad

    (iv) There has been a gradual reduction in private investment overseas from Britain each year since 1970

15. Which is the most fundamental explanation for Britain's worsening balance of trade situation in the 1970s?

    (a) Invisible items have not grown fast enough to keep pace with the deficit on visible items

    (b) Changing consumption patterns have stimulated demand for imported goods

    (c) Middle East oil producers have raised the price of oil

    (d) British exports have been uncompetitively priced

16. What is the effect of a budget surplus on the balance of payments?

    (a) It all depends on import elasticities

    (b) It all depends on whether the balance of payments is in surplus or deficit

    (c) It will help reduce a balance of payments deficit if other things remain the same

    (d) The effect is negligible as the two are not related

17. What is the effect of economic growth on the balance of payments?

 (a) It stimulates production, increases exports and therefore improves the balance of payments
 (b) It causes incomes to grow which increases demand for imports and therefore worsens the balance of payments
 (c) It all depends on whether the balance of payments is in surplus or deficit
 (d) It all depends on income elasticities for the products imported and exported

18. Which of the following items appear in the 'capital flow' section of the Balance of Payments Accounts?
 (i) Net transactions with I.M.F.
 (ii) Overseas investment in the U.K. private sector
 (iii) Interest, profits and dividends
 (iv) Exchange reserves in sterling, banking and other Money Market liabilities
 (v) Overseas currency borrowing
 (a) all of them   (c) ii, iv and v
 (b) all but i   (d) ii and v only

19. Which of the following statements about the balance of payments is true?
 (a) The Balance of Payments Accounts as a whole can never be in surplus or in deficit
 (b) Gold is the major element in the official reserves of the U.K.
 (c) A surplus on the 'capital flow' items of the balance of payments means that 'total official financing' must also be in surplus
 (d) The balance of payments on current account is synonymous with the balance of trade

20. Using the following information about unit costs of production of butter and machinery in two countries, Tintag and Grouvia:

	Tintag	Grouvia
Butter	10	9
Machinery	36	24

and assuming that 3 units of butter exchanges for 1 unit of machinery, which of the following would be true?

(a) Grouvia will export both butter and machinery to Tintag
(b) Tintag will import machinery and export butter
(c) Grouvia will import machinery and export butter
(d) Tintag will export both butter and machinery

21. An increase in the value of sterling balances in the U.K. balance of payments represents:

(a) a growth in Britain's purchasing power overseas
(b) an increase in Britain's reserves
(c) a strengthening of the position of sterling as a reserve currency
(d) an increase in the indebtedness of Britain to overseas sterling holders

22. Why should a government adopt a freer trade policy?

(i) To encourage international specialisation of factors of production
(ii) To allow international trade to reflect comparative cost advantages
(iii) To reduce the cost of commodities to consumers
(iv) To correct a balance of payments deficit
(v) To widen markets for commodities

(a) all but iv   (c) ii, iii and v
(b) v only   (d) for all the reasons

23. In 1974 Britain had its largest ever deficit on the current account of the balance of payments. What measures might the government use to try to correct the deficit?

(i) Borrow more from the I.M.F.
(ii) Introduce further controls on imports
(iii) Further devaluation
(iv) Subsidise industries which are attempting to export
(v) Run down our gold and foreign currency reserves

(a) all of them   (c) iv only
(b) ii, iii, and iv   (d) all but v

24. What effect would further devaluation have on:
    (i) the price of refrigerators sold in Britain?
    (ii) foreign holidays in the Algarve?

    (a) The price of ii would rise but i would be unaffected
    (b) The price of ii would rise and i would rise
    (c) The price of ii would fall and i would fall
    (d) The price of ii would be unaffected and i would rise

25. Why does the exchange of goods generally make consumers better off? Because:
    (i) it facilitates specialisation which makes it possible to produce goods more cheaply
    (ii) we exchange goods which have relatively low utility in this country for goods which have relatively higher utility
    (iii) the things we sell have a higher value than the things we buy

    (a) i only   (c) i, ii and iii
    (b) i and ii   (d) for none of these reasons

26. Match the following:
    (i) Absolute Cost Advantage for Grouvia
    (ii) Comparative Cost Advantage for Grouvia
    (iii) Equal cost for Tintag and Grouvia

	Grouvia	*Tintag*
(a)	100 units of butter or 80 units of machinery	50 units of butter or 60 units of machinery
(b)	100 units of butter or 80 units of machinery	50 units of butter or 40 units of machinery
(c)	100 units of butter or 50 units of machinery	50 units of butter or 30 units of machinery

18

FOREIGN EXCHANGE

1. Foreign Exchange is:
    (a) the exchange of goods and services between countries
    (b) the balance sheet of all transactions between countries
    (c) the currencies used to finance transactions between countries
    (d) all forms of international payments

2. The Foreign Exchange rate between two currencies will settle in a free market where:
    (a) the I.M.F. says it will
    (b) the central banks of the two countries say it will
    (c) the demand and supply of the two currencies is equal
    (d) the balance of payments between the countries is in equilibrium

3. Which of the following would produce a downward pressure on the sterling price of the Canadian dollar?
    (a) An increase in British demand for Canadian wheat
    (b) An expectation that the dollar would be devalued
    (c) A decrease in Canadian demand for British cars
    (d) None of these

4. The purchasing power parity theory argues that the long-term equilibrium exchange rate between two countries will be determined by the ratio of their internal purchasing powers. Which of the following criticisms of this theory is *not* valid?
    (a) Exchange rates are fixed by the I.M.F. which is not influenced by the theory
    (b) In the real world the operation of theory is distorted by policies of protection
    (c) Indirect taxation can be used by governments to ameliorate the effects of trade
    (d) In some countries international trade plays a very small part in affecting internal purchasing power

5. What is the main function of the Exchange Equalisation Account?

   (a) To arrange payment in settlement of the difference between the amount of currency entering or leaving a country in the accounting period
   (b) To raise the level of the exchange rate as high as possible
   (c) To buy or sell sterling in order to maintain a desirable exchange rate
   (d) To prevent any movement in the exchange rate

6. Other things being equal, which of the following would be likely to cause the dollar to appreciate in terms of the pound?

   (a) The U.S. President is summoned to appear before the Senate on an impeachment motion
   (b) Short-term capital moves from London to New York following a rise in the U.S. bank rate
   (c) The U.K. borrows money from the U.S.A.
   (d) I.C.I. sells a U.S. subsidiary and places the money through the London money market

7. If the Exchange Equalisation Account does not wish the exchange rate for sterling to fall, which of the following would lead it to buy sterling?

   (a) A large increase in the cost of Britain's imports
   (b) A movement of hot money into London
   (c) Germany agrees to contribute fully to the E.E.C. fund for development areas
   (d) None of these

8. Britain now operates a floating exchange rate policy. In these circumstances, which of the following will bring about a short term appreciation in the exchange value of sterling?

   (a) British citizens buy shares in the Lockheed Aircraft Company
   (b) The Bank of England converts its foreign currency reserves into gold
   (c) The government repays its debt to the I.M.F.
   (d) The Ford Motor Company buys up its British subsidiary

9. In 1973 the rate of exchange between the pound and the dollar changed from £1 = $2.40 to £1 = $2.20. Which of the following offers a possible explanation for this change?

(a) An increase in British interest rates
(b) A rise in the U.S. rate of unemployment
(c) An improvement in U.S. balance of payments
(d) A rise in the U.S. rate of inflation

10. The main advantage of a fixed exchange rate for a currency is that:

(a) it prevents all speculation
(b) it enables traders to know what the price of foreign goods will be
(c) it makes it much easier to balance payments
(d) it makes it unnecessary to support the rate from our reserves

11. Britain announces a heavy deficit on its balance of payments. If the authorities make no attempt to interfere with the normal workings of market forces, what is most likely to happen to the exchange rate?

(a) The balance of payments has no effect one way or the other on the exchange rate
(b) As long as Britain has ample gold and foreign exchange reserves, there will be no effect
(c) Britain, in borrowing to settle the payments deficit, will attract funds to the country and so raise the exchange rate
(d) A payments deficit means that imports are attractively cheap and exports too dear, and so the exchange rate must fall to compensate for this

12. When the exchange rate between the £ and the $ is 1 : 2.5 Britain sells 10,000 teddy bears to the United States at £1 each. If the demand for teddy bears in the U.S. is unitary, how many teddy bears will be sold if the rate changes to 1 : 2, all other things remaining the same?

(a) 7,500   (b) 10,000   (c) 12,500   (d) 25,000

13. How would this affect teddy bear manufacturers in this country?
    (a) They would increase their revenue
    (b) They would decrease their revenue
    (c) There would be no change in their revenue
    (d) There is not enough information to decide

14. If the manufacturers decide to increase the price of teddy bears to £2 at the same time as the exchange rate changes (but all other things remain the same) how would the balance of trade be affected?
    (a) It would be improved
    (b) It would be worsened
    (c) It would be unaffected
    (d) There is not enough information to decide

15. Until recently sterling and dollars were the foremost of a very small number of reserve currencies. They are reserve currencies because:
    (a) they are widely accepted and held by countries to make payments
    (b) they are accepted by the I.M.F. as the only legal tender currencies
    (c) they are freely exchangeable in gold
    (d) they are the basis of the creation of S.D.Rs.

16. What is the real importance of S.D.Rs. in international payments?
    (a) They have solved the problem of international liquidity
    (b) They are accepted by central banks in settlement of debts
    (c) They are everywhere acceptable in place of gold
    (d) Their introduction has effectively reduced the price of gold

17. *True/False?*
    (i) G.A.T.T. is mainly concerned with making trade freer
    (ii) I.M.F. is mainly concerned with making international monetary settlements easier
    (iii) I.B.R.D. is mainly concerned with supplying funds to industrialised nations
    (iv) The Upper Volta Agreement is a common market arrangement between Communist countries

18. Which of the following has no part in the operation of the I.M.F.?

   (a) The total *tranche* position
   (b) The Gold Quota
   (c) The adjustment of exchange rates
   (d) The promotion of common market schemes

19. Match the international monetary terms with the most suitable definition:

   (i) Sterling balances   (a) A medium of international short-term money markets

   (ii) Euro-currencies   (b) A medium for the settlement of international debts

   (iii) Special Drawing Rights   (c) Claims on currency holdings with short term maturity

   (iv) Negotiable Certificates of Deposit   (d) Claims for foreign exchange by sterling area countries

20. The most rapidly rising element in Britain's import bill is that for manufactured items. If the demand for these items is elastic, what would be the effect of a devaluation of the pound on the import bill?

   (a) It would increase
   (b) It would decrease
   (c) It would remain the same
   (d) It would depend on the elasticity of other items in the import bill

19

GOVERNMENT ECONOMIC POLICY

1. What are the main objectives of the government in its economic policy?
   - (i) To promote a favourable growth of G.N.P.
   - (ii) To reduce the level of unemployment
   - (iii) To raise the standard of living of the population
   - (iv) To produce a long term surplus on the balance of payments
   - (v) To control population growth to maximise output per head
   - (vi) To increase the level of savings
   - (a) all of them
   - (b) all but vi
   - (c) i, ii, iii and vi
   - (d) i, ii and iii

2. What was the main effect of the work of J. M. Keynes on government economic policy?
   - (a) He brought policy out of the age of *laissez-faire* into the age of government intervention
   - (b) He introduced the idea of economic planning
   - (c) He advocated the use of government expenditure to maintain the level of aggregate demand
   - (d) He demonstrated that control of inflation was the key to successful management of the economy

3. Economists advocate economic planning for many reasons. Which of the following carries most weight?
   Planning enables the government to:
   - (a) engineer a more balanced growth of G.N.P.
   - (b) remove differences in economic performance between regions
   - (c) eliminate the problems associated with 'Stop-Go'
   - (d) balance external payments

4. Industrialists support advocates of economic planning because:
   (a) They do better when the G.N.P. is increasing
   (b) They can gear their policies to those of the government
   (c) They can use the information to speculate on the Stock Exchange
   (d) It gives them an advantage over foreign competitors

5. *True/False?*
   (i) The government finances about two-thirds of all scientific and technological research
   (ii) The government accounts for about two-thirds of all fixed investment in the country
   (iii) Government expenditure accounts for less than one-third of the G.N.P.
   (iv) Taxation takes over 40% of income out of circulation

6. Why do we expect the government to provide a wide range of social services instead of leaving it to private enterprise to provide them?
   (i) Only the government has a big enough labour force and can afford to employ it
   (ii) Only the government has sufficient expertise
   (iii) If left to the profit motive the services could only be supplied at a much higher price
   (iv) Private enterprise is not efficient enough
   (v) In this way duplication of resources is avoided

   (a) v only   (c) ii, iii and v
   (b) iii and v   (d) all of them

7. Statement I. The nation would benefit from certain private enterprises being brought into public ownership
   Statement II. Nationalised enterprises charge lower prices and so the real cost to the nation is reduced
   (a) Both statements are true
   (b) Statement I is true and Statement II false
   (c) State II is true and Statement I false
   (d) Both statements are false

8. Why does the government wish to control inflation? Because:
   - (a) all sections of the community are made worse off
   - (b) the real burden of the National Debt is increased
   - (c) it causes the terms of trade to move against us
   - (d) it discourages saving

9. Which of the following is most likely to benefit from inflation?
   - (a) A pensioner
   - (b) A schoolteacher
   - (c) A householder with a mortgage
   - (d) A holder of gilt edged securities

10. *True/False?*
    - (i) The deficit on the balance of payments in 1973 was higher than in any previous year
    - (ii) The number unemployed in 1971 was higher than in any previous year since the war
    - (iii) The growth of the money supply in 1973 was greater than in any previous year
    - (iv) The rate of rise in prices in U.K. in 1973 was higher than that in any other European country

11. Although governments have operated control of prices and incomes, there has traditionally been considerable reluctance to use such direct controls because:
    - (a) monetary weapons give a finer degree of control
    - (b) they interfere with the free working of the system of allocating resources and so increase inefficiency
    - (c) fiscal measures, particularly reductions in taxation, are politically more attractive
    - (d) direct controls are the weapons of a planned economy and therefore unworkable in a free enterprise economy

12. Professor Paish has argued the need for a policy designed to produce a margin of productive potential. The object of this would be:

    (a) to allow production to expand without producing inflationary pressures
    (b) to stimulate a much higher rate of growth
    (c) to improve industrial relations by raising marginal wage rates
    (d) to allow this margin to be used in stimulating exports

13. The government currently faces the problems of:

    (i) a high rate of inflation
    (ii) a low rate of growth
    (iii) a fairly high level of unemployment
    (iv) a huge balance of payments deficit

    Which of the following, if any, is most likely to be effective in such a situation?

    (a) Measures to reduce the money supply
    (b) Measures to reduce the level of aggregate demand
    (c) Measures to increase the level of production
    (d) Measures to increase the money supply

14. During the inter-war depression the mean features were:

    (i) a very high level of unemployment
    (ii) very low interest rates
    (iii) falling prices
    (iv) a deficit on the balance of trade

    Which of the following measures should the government have adopted to deal with these problems?

    (a) A reduction of the money supply to further reduce prices and thus increase demand through consumption
    (b) An increase in government expenditure to raise the level of demand
    (c) An increase in taxation to fund social security payments and thus increase demand through consumption
    (d) An increase in bank rate to attract more funds and thus increase demand through investment

15. Which of the following is most likely to increase the National Debt?
    (a) A balance of payments deficit
    (b) An increase in income tax
    (c) A rise in long-term government borrowing
    (d) A rise in the standard of living

16. Why do governments not attempt to pay off the National Debt? Because:
    (a) it would not be possible to do so
    (b) there would be little to be gained by a mere transfer of resources
    (c) it would have a very serious effect on the balance of payments
    (d) Britain's gold and foreign currency resources are insufficient

17. *True/False?*
    (i) In 1973 interest rates in Britain were higher than they had ever been
    (ii) In the ten years up to 1973 Britain had the lowest growth rate of all industrialised countries in Europe
    (ii) In 1974 the pound was worth about 10p when compared with the pound in 1874
    (iv) The National Debt is approximately equal in size to the National Income

18. *True/False?*
    (i) Since 1970 rates of tax have been reduced but total tax revenue increased
    (ii) Since 1970 the increase in retail prices has been greater than the increase in average earnings
    (iii) There have been several occasions since 1970 when vacancies have exceeded numbers unemployed
    (iv) The balance of payments has been in deficit every year since 1970

19. Which of the following monetary measures has been used by the government since September 1971?

    (i) Bank Rate   (ii) Ceilings on lending
    (iii) Special Deposits   (iv) Directives to the banks
    (v) Funding   (vi) Open Market Operations

    (a) all of them   (c) all but ii
    (b) all but i   (d) iii, iv, v and vi

20. Which of the following are measures of physical control?

    (i) Import and Export licensing
    (ii) Building licences
    (iii) Price controls
    (iv) Incomes controls
    (v) Control of hire purchase
    (vi) Rationing

    (a) all of them   (c) iii, iv and vi only
    (b) all but v   (d) iii and iv only

21. To solve which of the following problems would it be appropriate for the government to increase the size of the budget deficit?

    (a) A fall in the value of money
    (b) Shortage of government funds
    (c) Inequality of incomes
    (d) A fall in the level of employment

22. Which of the following would you recommend most strongly to a Chancellor who wanted to reduce inequality in the distribution of personal wealth?

    (a) A wealth tax
    (b) A tax on luxury items
    (c) A tax on income derived from wealth holding
    (d) A tax on capital gains